STREIGHT'S FOILED RAID ON THE WESTERN & ATLANTIC RAILROAD

Emma Sansom's Courage and Nathan Bedford Forrest's Pursuit

BRANDON H. BECK

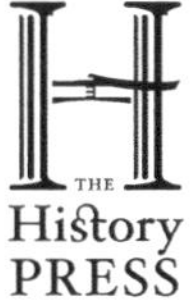

Published by The History Press
Charleston, SC
www.historypress.net

First published 2016

Manufactured in the United States

ISBN 978.1.62619.862.3

Library of Congress Control Number: 2015957670

Dedication

In 1896, Dr. John Allan Wyeth, preparing his biography of Forrest, *Life of Lieutenant General Forrest* (1899), wrote to Emma Sansom, who "rode with General Forrest." He asked for her help in recounting the day at Black Creek, May 2, 1863, thirty-three years earlier. He published her account in his biography and dedicated the biography to her.

In 2014, I wrote to Emma's great-grandson Larry Johnson, asking him to help me recount her story. Over the course of a year, he gave me invaluable information. As Dr. Wyeth dedicated his book to Emma, I am grateful to be able to dedicate this book to Larry Johnson and his family.

Contents

Acknowledgements

I'm very grateful to the following people for their help with this book:

Tommy Barber, Duluth, Georgia, former chair, Georgia Civil War Commission, for keeping me up to date on Atlanta 1862–63.

Melissa Beck, for typing and formatting the manuscript and many suggestions for improvement.

Civil War Trust, for permission to use the Streight's Raid map from one of its two markers at Hog Mountain Battlefield in Alabama.

Danny Crownover, Gadsden, Alabama, president and executive director, Etowah Historical Society & Heritage Museum, for sources, a guided tour and leading me to Larry Johnson, Emma Sansom's great-grandson.

Norman Dasinger Jr., Gadsden, Alabama, Streight Raid tour guide with the Civil War Education Association, for a guided tour and the timeline included in this book and for his interpretation of the action at Blount's Plantation.

Jim Dowdle, DVM, Columbus, Mississippi, for insight into the character and health of mules.

Kevin Grades, archivist, Gadsden Public Library, for sources and references, particularly in the Gadsden newspaper archives.

Gail Gunter, head librarian, Fant Memorial Library, Mississippi University for Women, Columbus, Mississippi, for finding all of my inter-library loan requests.

Larry Johnson, Arlington, Texas, great-grandson of Emma (Sansom) and Christopher Johnson (see dedication page).

Henry McElroy, Maringouin, Louisiana, for sharing family papers.

Bob Price, Alpharetta, Georgia, historian, photographer and tour guide.

Elisa Shizak, Caledonia, Mississippi, and the Stephen D. Lee chapter of the United Daughters of the Confederacy, for genealogical research into the Streight family.

Amy Vedra, director, Reference Services, Indiana Historical Society, for sources and references.

Jim Woodrick, director of Mississippi Department of Archives and History, Jackson, Mississippi, for references and the Warren Grabau manuscript (see bibliography).

Robert Willett's *The Lightning Mule Brigade: Abel Streight's 1863 Raid into Alabama* is the indispensible "first read" on Streight's Raid.

Introduction

A Western & Atlantic timetable for March 1861 shows how important this 138-mile railroad from Atlanta, Georgia, to Chattanooga, Tennessee, had become. It linked the second and third most important railroad centers in the Confederacy, Atlanta and Chattanooga, with the most important, the capital city of Richmond. At Atlanta, there were connections for Montgomery, Macon, and Augusta. Coming north, there were connections at Cartersville for the Etowah Ironworks, at Kingston for Rome, and at Dalton, for the East Tennessee & Georgia. At Chattanooga, there were connections for Memphis, Nashville, and Richmond.

These connections, along with Atlanta's growth and manufacturing capacity, made the line an important contributor to the Confederate war effort. In 1862 and 1863, its tracks were the final miles of the Confederacy's two largest troop movements by rail. Until 1864, it helped supply both of the Confederacy's field armies, the Army of Northern Virginia and the Army of Tennessee. The Union tried twice to break or cripple it. The first attempt was in 1862, a bold effort to isolate and seize Chattanooga. The second was in 1863, part of a coordinated offensive that had Vicksburg as its ultimate objective. In the first, the W&A successfully defended itself against the Andrews Raiders in the Georgia locomotive chase. In the second, General Nathan Bedford Forrest pursued and then captured the raiding force of Colonel Abel D. Streight. Both raids involved strategic planning on the highest levels—that of Major Don Carlos Buell, commander of the Union's Army of the Ohio; Joseph E. Johnston, commander of the Confederacy's

Department of the West; Ulysses S. Grant, commanding the Army of the Tennessee; President Abraham Lincoln; William Rosecrans, Buell's successor; and Braxton Bragg, commander of the Army of Tennessee.

But the most important figures in the telling of these stories are either civilians or officers without prewar military experience. These include a Kentucky smuggler and spy, a determined and angry W&A Railroad conductor, an Indianapolis author and publisher, a Memphis slave trader and military genius, an Alabama mail carrier, and a fifteen-year-old girl living with her mother and sister on the banks of Black Creek in Gadsden, Alabama. The tie binding them all is the W&A Railroad.

Streight's Raid and Forrest's Pursuit: Timeline

April 6	Streight's Independent Provisional Brigade leaves Murfreesboro, Tennessee.
April 11	Streight's troops leave Nashville on the Cumberland River for Palmyra, Tennessee.
April 15	Streight arrives at Fort Henry on the Tennessee River. Dodge's cavalry leaves Corinth, Mississippi.
April 16	Dodge's force arrives at Great Bear Creek, Alabama.
April 17	Streight leaves Fort Henry on the Tennessee River for Eastport, Mississippi. Dodge crosses Great Bear Creek and engages Colonel P.D. Roddey at Barton's Station, Alabama.
April 19	Streight arrives at Eastport and rides to meet Dodge at Great Bear Creek. Mules stampede at Eastport.
April 22	Streight and Dodge join forces at Great Bear Creek.
April 23	Dodge advances on Tuscumbia and arrives there late in the day with Streight in the rear. Forrest is ordered to cross the Tennessee River and reinforce Roddey.
April 24	Dodge skirmishes with Roddey at Leighton.
April 26	Streight leaves Dodge at Tuscumbia, heads south toward Russellville and then east to Moulton, Alabama.

April 27–28	Dodge moves from Tuscumbia for Town Creek and clashes with Roddey. Forrest reinforces Roddey.
April 28	Streight arrives at Moulton at 3:00 p.m.
April 29	Dodge moves back toward Tuscumbia, and Forrest deploys from Courtland.
April 30	Forrest attacks Streight at Day's Gap, Crooked Creek, and Hog Mountain.
May 1	Streight passes through Blountsville with Forrest in pursuit.
May 2	Forrest leaves Walnut Grove. Streight nears Gadsden with Forrest in pursuit. Emma Sansom shows Forrest the low water ford across Black Creek. Both Streight and Forrest pass through Gadsden and Turkeytown and clash at Blount's Plantation. John Wisdom rides to Rome, arriving near midnight.
May 3	Streight crosses Chattooga River on Dykes' Bridge, followed by Forrest. Streight passes through Cedar Bluff with Forrest following. Streight halts near the Lawrence House. Streight surrenders.
May 4	Streight's men moved to Kingston and then Atlanta.
May 5–6	Forrest moves west to Shelbyville, Tennessee.
May 7	Death of General Earl Van Dorn.
May 10	Death of Stonewall Jackson.

Connections at Atlanta and Chattanooga

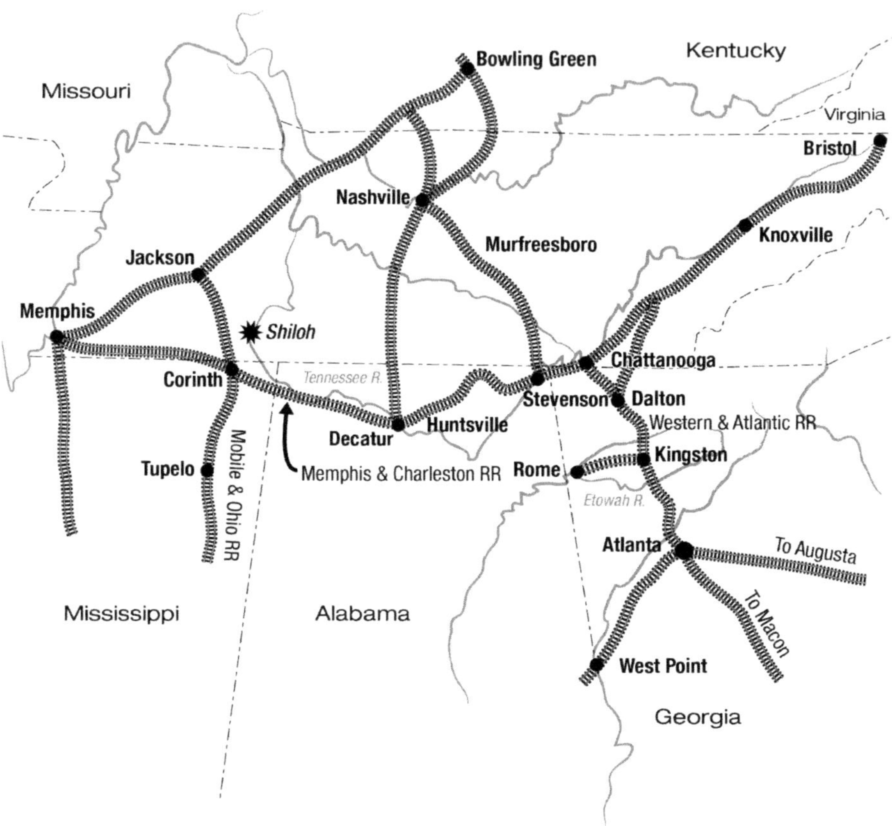

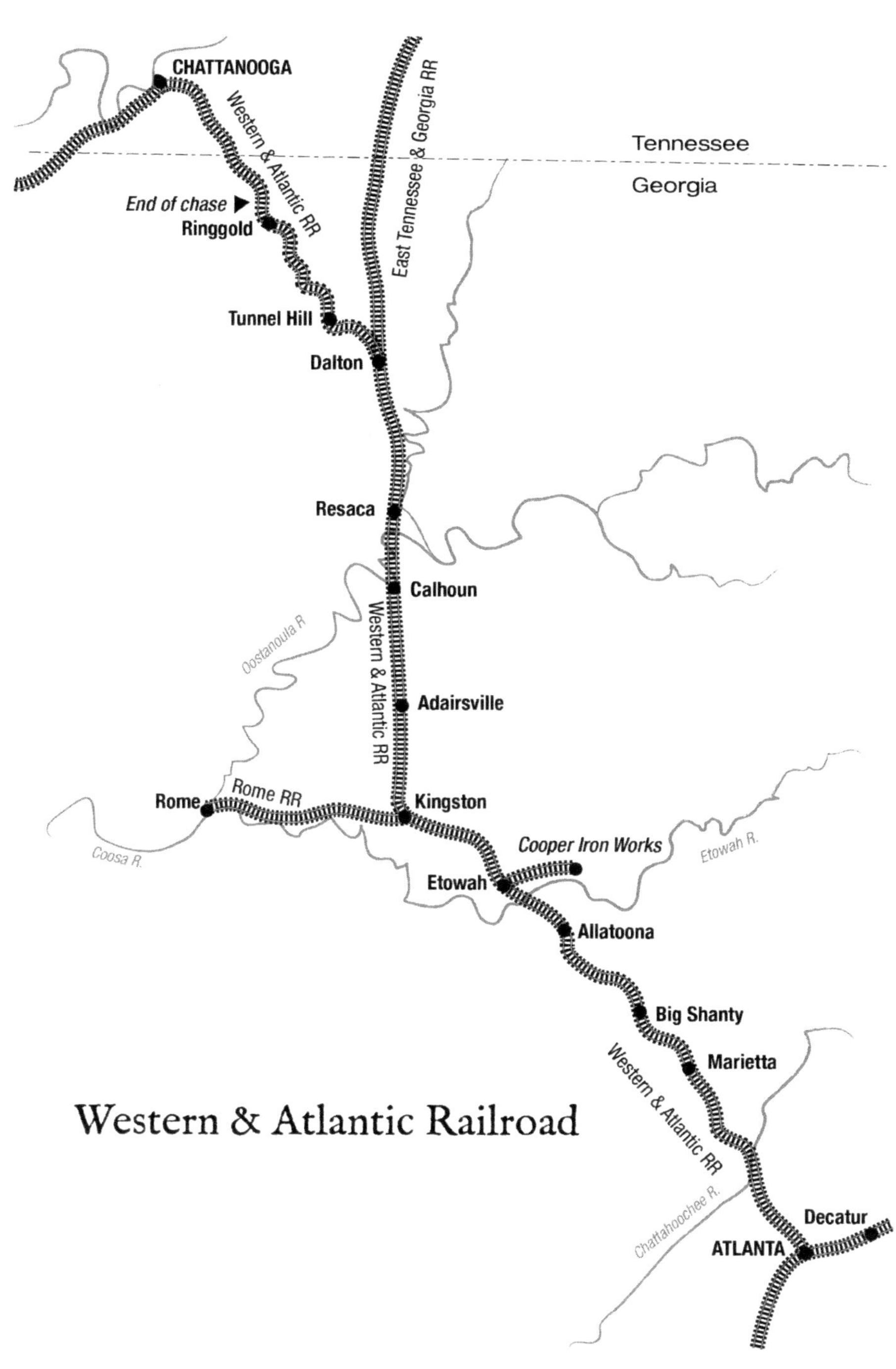

Western & Atlantic Railroad

Chapter 1

The Western & Atlantic Railroad: Zero Milepost to Chattanooga

In 1836, the future vice president of the Confederate States of America rose to make his first speech in the Georgia legislature. Alexander H. Stephens, twenty-four, spoke forcefully in favor of the state chartering what became the state-owned Western & Atlantic. "I was amongst the most zealous advocates," he recalled. "My object was to show the great utility of the road as an ultimate outlet to the trade and travel of the great Northwest."

There was fierce opposition. One opponent mocked the line as "beginning nowhere and ending nowhere, over mountains too steep for a spider to climb up." Another critic, either unfamiliar with railroad terminology or too beside himself to recall the term "main trunk line," asked, "What do you call it, Mister Speaker? The 'main snout,' I believe?"

Nevertheless, the enabling bill passed on December 21, 1836. Stephens thought it might be "the most important day in Georgia history since the beginning of the present century."[1]

The W&A became a trunk line, linking Georgia with the Tennessee River. Although neither of its terminals, Atlanta or Chattanooga, figured in the line's name, it was largely responsible for the sudden growth of both cities.[2] The company placed its Zero Milepost in Terminus, Georgia, which soon became Marthasville and, finally, Atlanta.[3]

Colonel Stephen H. Long, the line's chief engineer, surveyed the initial route between May 1837 and November 1840. The northern terminal was first placed at Rossville Landing, on the Tennessee River, near Chattanooga.

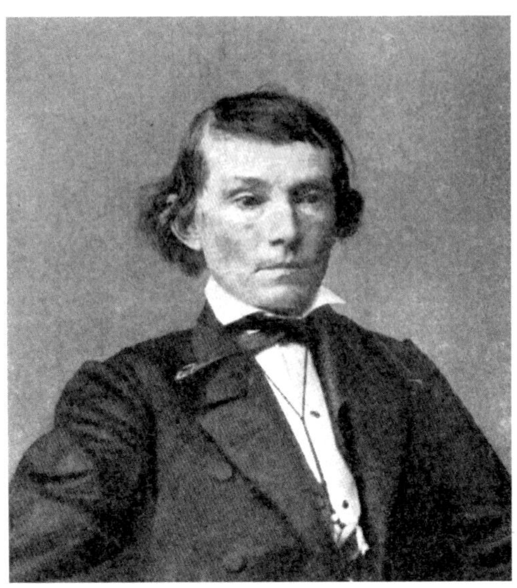

Alexander H. Stephens (1817–1883). Stephens' first speech in the Georgia legislature in 1836 was in favor of Georgia chartering a state-owned railroad, the Western & Atlantic. He served as vice president of the Confederate States of America and, after the War, as governor of Georgia. *From* The Photographic History of the Civil War in Ten Volumes, Semi-Centennial Memorial Edition, *Francis T. Miller, Editor-in-Chief, New York, The Review of Reviews Co., 1911.*

The Panic of 1837 slowed and then halted construction of the line. The state came close to pulling out of the project, but after Charles Garrett became chief engineer, the work went steadily forward. One of the first trains was a Christmas special from Atlanta to Marietta in 1842. The railroad won another legislative victory for funding in 1847 and, by 1859, was operating as far north as Dalton, Georgia. The route did not go west to Rome, but in 1849, the Rome Railroad joined the Western & Atlantic at Kingston.[4]

One obstacle remained: Chetoogeta Mountain, just north of Dalton. Until 1849, passengers and freight had to go over the mountain by wagon. The great tunnel, Tunnel Hill, 1,477 feet long, was opened for its first train on May 9, 1849. The tunnel put the Western & Atlantic through to Ringgold and Chattanooga.[5] After passing Ringgold, the line rounded the northern end of Missionary Ridge to reach the Western & Atlantic depot at Ninth and Market Streets.[6]

The right of way, 138 miles long, was graded for double track, but the railroad remained single track with passing sidings through the War. Adairsville was the halfway point, just over 60 miles from Atlanta and Chattanooga.[7] A typical southbound run required a little over eight hours. The surveyors preferred curves, narrow and sharp, to grades. The result was "the crookedest road under the sun."[8]

By 1859, the locomotive roster included fifty-two engines, some of which were leased to other lines. (The General and the Texas joined the roster in 1855.) There were also fifty-two passenger and baggage cars and over six hundred freight cars of all types. Also that year, the line showed a profit of $450,000, most of which went into maintenance and improvement of the right of way.

The line had a marked effect on the region it served, stimulating population growth and the production of cotton.[9] The most obvious result was on the growth of Atlanta and Chattanooga. Atlanta's population increased fourfold in the 1850s, rising to just under ten thousand by the time of the War. There was a single switchyard and train shed for all the railroads entering the city. The Western & Atlantic shops "were the largest and best equipped in the city."[10] Atlanta was the most important railroad hub in the Deep South, with an unrivalled manufacturing capacity.[11] The War brought Confederate commissary and quartermaster officers to the city.[12] By 1862, "Atlanta was dominated by the needs of Confederate military forces."[13]

The Western & Atlantic was the link—vital and irreplaceable—between Atlanta and Montgomery, Macon, Columbus, and Augusta, and also between Confederate forces in both Virginia and Tennessee. At Chattanooga, the line connected with the Memphis & Charleston, described as the "vertebrae of the Confederacy," which linked that city with both Memphis and, via Knoxville and Lynchburg, with Virginia. The Memphis & Charleston operated east of Stevenson, Alabama, into Chattanooga, over the tracks of the Nashville & Chattanooga Railroad.

Railroads and the War utterly transformed Chattanooga: "Every day and into the night, trains passed through heavy laden with men and material, transporting arms from the arsenals of Georgia to supply Confederate forces in the northeast."[14] But Atlanta was safe only if the Confederates could hold Chattanooga, and Chattanooga, along with most of the Confederate west, was vulnerable almost from the very beginning of the War.

Chapter 2

Defending the Western & Atlantic Against James J. Andrews and General Don Carlos Buell

The defense of the Confederacy between the Appalachians and the Mississippi River—i.e., the west—began to unravel in February 1862. The loss of Fort Henry on the Tennessee River and Fort Donelson on the Cumberland River turned both rivers into "aquatic daggers aimed at the heartland of the Confederacy."[15] Nashville, on the Cumberland, was the first Confederate state capital to fall into Union hands. Its loss was a direct threat to Chattanooga; it made the Nashville & Chattanooga Railroad a potential line of advance and supply for General Don Carlos Buell's Army of the Ohio.

In April 1862, however, the largest part of Buell's army was heading west to join Major General U.S. Grant's Army of the Tennessee at Pittsburg Landing on the Tennessee River. After the Union victory at Shiloh on April 6–7, Corinth, rather than either Vicksburg or Chattanooga, became the Union's next objective. Chattanooga, still unfortified and only lightly garrisoned, seemed safe. But not all of Buell's army had gone west. He left behind troops in the Cumberland Gap, at Nashville, and, most critically, Major General Ormsby M. Mitchel's four-thousand-man division at Shelbyville, Tennessee.[16]

Mitchel's orders were to guard the bridges along the Nashville & Chattanooga Railroad. But his orders also held out the enticing possibility of seizing "the Memphis and Charleston Railroad when the opportunity offered" either at Decatur or Huntsville, Alabama.[17]

Mitchel saw in these orders and in Buell's absence the opportunity to do much more than guard one railroad and block another. He was

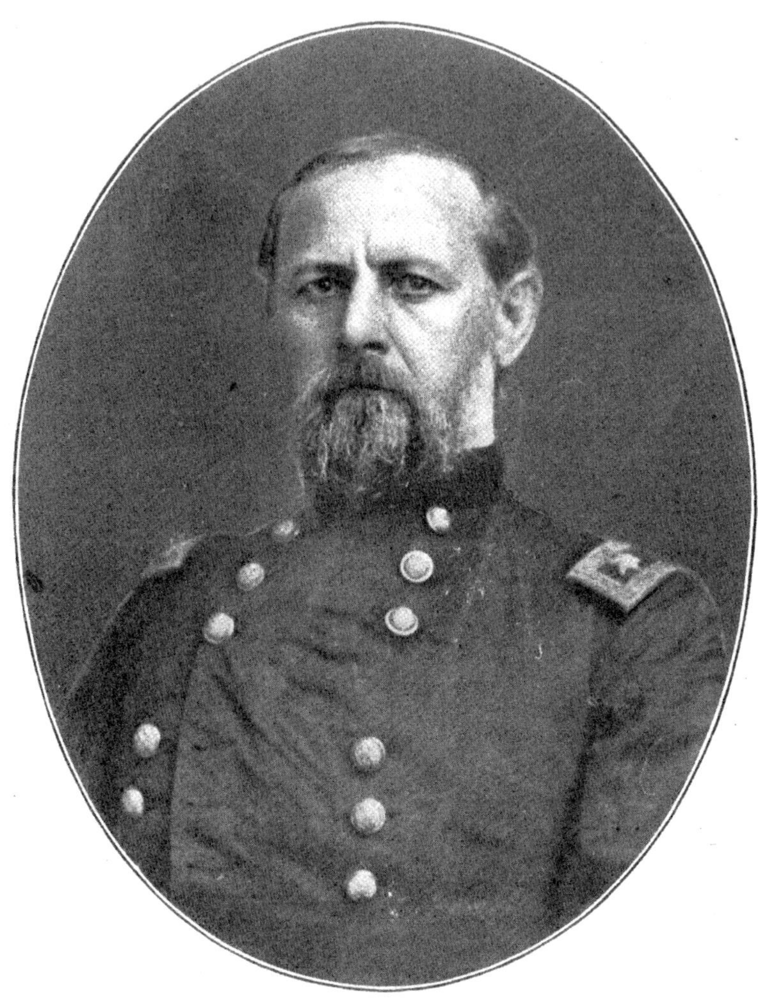

General Don Carlos Buell (1818–1896). Commanding the Army of the Ohio (later, Cumberland), Buell occupied Nashville after the fall of Fort Donelson, but he was unable to seriously threaten Chattanooga. He was relieved in October 1862 after forcing Bragg to retreat from Kentucky to Murfreesboro, Tennessee. *From* The Photographic History of the Civil War in Ten Volumes, Semi-Centennial Memorial Edition, *Francis T. Miller, Editor-in-Chief, New York, The Review of Reviews Co., 1911.*

intrigued by a bold, imaginative, and, to him, low-risk plan put forward by James J. Andrews, "a spy in the employ of General Buell."[18]

Andrews' plan held out an alluring prospect: to "press into the heart of the enemy's country as far as possible, occupying strategical points before they were adequately defended."[19] The lure was Chattanooga—to take it while it was lightly defended and before the Confederates were aware of the danger. Mitchel's division would occupy Huntsville and then advance east along the railroad, cutting Chattanooga off from the Confederate force at Corinth. On the same day, April 11, Andrews and his men, another civilian, and twenty-four soldiers (at least two missed the train) from Mitchel's 2nd, 21st, and 33rd Ohio, dressed as civilians, would board and then steal a W&A train from Atlanta headed for Chattanooga. Cutting telegraph wires, lifting rails, and burning bridges behind them, they would cut Chattanooga off from Atlanta, completing its isolation and laying it open for Mitchel's advance. Andrews would run his train through Chattanooga and somehow get onto the westbound main line, along which the raiders would meet Mitchel's advancing troops.[20]

April 11 was the appointed day. Mitchel was on time; he occupied Huntsville and moved to within thirty miles of Chattanooga. Andrews was late. Thinking that heavy rain would delay Mitchel, Andrews didn't strike until April 12. Sergeant (later Reverend) William Pittenger of the 2nd Ohio Volunteer Infantry, who was with Andrews, called this "a natural but most lamentable error of judgment." April 12 brought both heavy rain and abnormally heavy southbound traffic on the Western & Atlantic.[21] On April 11, the W&A was a single-track railroad operating in peacetime. But Mitchel's advance meant that, on April 12, the W&A was on a wartime footing. Dispatchers in Chattanooga, well aware of Georgia governor Joseph Brown's fiercely protective policy for his state's railroad, reacted to Mitchel's advance by sending rolling stock south—"extra" trains—necessitating more and longer "meets." Andrews could not have known the new schedule, nor would he have train orders, giving him priority over the "extra" trains.

Andrews and his men boarded the regularly scheduled morning train to Chattanooga at Marietta. It was a "mixed" train, with a few boxcars immediately behind the tender. The train's conductor was William Fuller. No man on the W&A payroll could have been more dangerous to Andrews than Fuller.

Fuller's train left Atlanta on time, behind the engine General. When the train made its regular stop for breakfast at Big Shanty, today's Kennesaw, Fuller and his engine crew joined the true passengers in the Lacy Hotel dining room, leaving the General simmering and unguarded. Andrews' men lingered outside. They would have been the last to enter the restaurant. But suddenly, moving fast, they uncoupled the boxcars from the trailing passenger cars. The soldiers climbed into the boxcars, while Andrews and the new engine crew climbed up into the cab. The fireman stoked his fire, and the engineer took off his brake and opened his throttle. In his haste to get underway, however, he gave the cylinders too much steam, so that even with a lighter train, the General's drivers slipped and spun before he could pull back on the throttle to gain sure footing.[22] When Fuller and his engineer heard the ensuing sharp exhaust of their train starting, they rushed outside to find it gone. Without hesitation, Fuller, the engineer, and another W&A official set off in pursuit—on foot. On foot at first, then on a pole car, then a switch engine—the Yonah, taken over at Etowah—and on foot again before reaching a second and then a third engine, Fuller would not give up. In a manner of speaking, he didn't relent until June 7, when he saw Andrews hang in Atlanta. Throughout April 12, he stayed close enough behind the "engine thieves" to come within reach of them at Kingston, sixty miles north.

In terms of track work, Kingston was the largest station on the line. There were passing sidings for W&A trains and a wye for turning the Rome train so that it could run engine-first westbound to Rome. On April 12, the train from Rome, behind the William R. Smith, was just in when Andrews arrived.[23]

Andrews expected one meet here and two farther on. He had concocted a very plausible story that would explain Fuller's absence and his presence. Cutting the telegraph wire behind him as he came north and "lying like a backwoods' politician"[24] in Kingston, he told the W&A men that Confederate authorities in Atlanta had taken over Fuller's train and loaded the boxcars with powder for General Beauregard at Corinth. He was charged with conducting the train through. Fuller's regularly scheduled train would be along soon.

The southbound arrived in Kingston on schedule, apparently giving Andrews the main line. But to his bitter chagrin, the road was not clear; a red flag on the rear of the southbound train meant that Andrews would have to wait for one, and then a second, southbound extra—rolling stock headed for safety. Andrews' story, plausible on its face, was perfectly suited to his growing frustration and impatience. He was not yet aware that he was being pursued. But the delay, which stretched to more than an hour, was agonizing.

When the line finally cleared, the General started its train, rapidly gaining speed. But as Pittenger and the other men huddled in the boxcars soon learned, "we were not many minutes ahead."[25] Also, unfortunately for the raiders, it began to rain.[26]

Andrews stopped his train four miles from Kingston, just south of Adairsville, to lift a rail. But as Pittenger wrote, "We had no good instruments for track raising as we had intended rather to rely upon fire."[27] They had only a single iron bar. They struggled mightily for long minutes before finally snapping the rail. It was then that they heard the whistle—from the south. It was Fuller. He had commandeered the William R. Smith from the Rome train at Kingston. Andrews now knew he was being pursued. Pursuit behind—and two oncoming southbound trains ahead! Steaming on, Andrews met and cleared the first southbound train, behind the Texas, at Adairsville.[28]

The Texas then started its train and continued on to the south. Andrews did not wait at Adairsville for the next southbound train but gambled that he could make Calhoun, the next stop north, before the southbound train left there. It was either that or collide with it head-on. He threw caution to the wind, running at nearly sixty miles per hour, protected only by a screaming whistle on unballasted and curving track suited for no more than half that speed. That either engine—the General or, later, the Texas—stayed on the tracks is nearly miraculous.

Fuller, meanwhile, was on foot again. He had stopped the William R. Smith before it came upon the broken rail. Two miles south of Adairsville, he and Andrew Murphy, a railroad official, were able to flag down the oncoming Texas. Climbing up into the cab, Fuller ordered the engineer to back the train into the siding at Adairsville, uncouple from the train, regain the main line, and set off in pursuit in reverse. Fuller watched the track ahead from the tender. Quickly, the Texas' speed rose to match the General's.

The southbound train was just pulling out of Calhoun when Andrews came into sight. Andrews endured another agonizing delay for the time it took to persuade its engineer to take the siding and give him the main line. He stopped again beyond Calhoun to cut the telegraph wire and lift a rail. But this time the men could neither break nor lift the rail. "If one rail could now be lifted we would be in a few minutes at Oostenaula [*sic*] Bridge [leaving] the enemy absolutely powerless."[29] But they couldn't lift it; they could only bend it. "Had they been equipped with a few proper tools for lifting spikes, they would have made themselves safe from Fuller's pursuit, but the need had not been anticipated when they had been thinking only of burning bridges."[30] The Texas' whistle was screaming behind them.

Fuller stopped long enough at Calhoun to pick up a telegrapher. At Dalton, the telegrapher succeeded in getting most of a warning message through to Chattanooga before the raiders cut the wire again.

The bridge Andrews most wanted to burn crossed the Oostanaula at Resaca. It could not be easily repaired or rebuilt. But the rain had been too heavy and the time had grown too short for the bridge to catch fire in the time Andrews had. Fuller "pushed right through the smoke."[31]

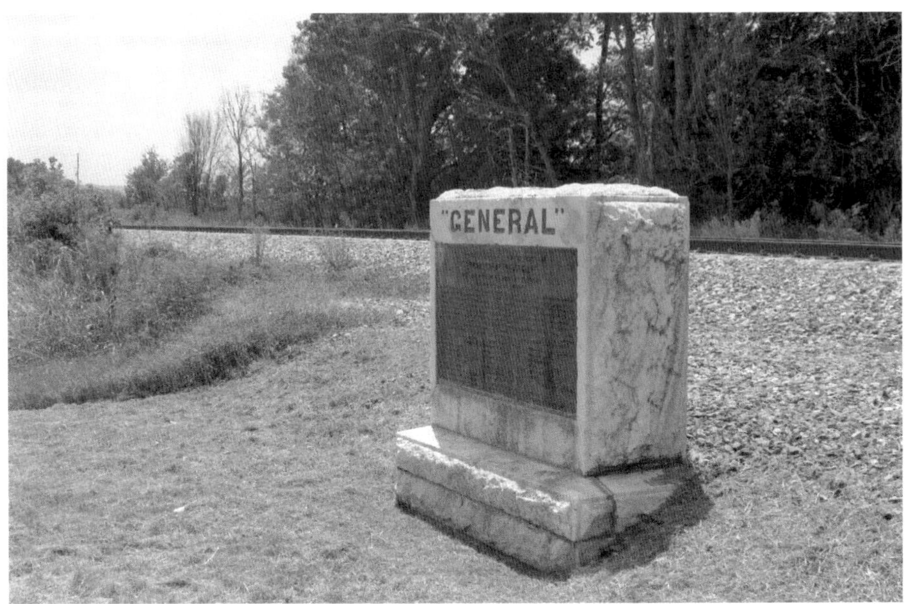

It was here that Andrews disbanded his men and abandoned the General. The marker is at railroad milepost 116.2 on Georgia Route 151, just north of Ringgold. *Bob Price, photographer.*

Andrews pressed on. There were smaller bridges over Chickamauga Creek north of Ringgold, and he had no choice but to try to get far enough ahead to be able to destroy one of them. But the Texas had somehow stayed on the tracks while racing over the bent rail. Andrews' train, now down to a single boxcar (two had been dropped), rumbled through Tunnel Hill and Dalton with Fuller close behind. But the General was low on both wood and water and began losing speed. Three miles beyond Ringgold, eighteen miles short of Chattanooga, Andrews gave up the mission. He disbanded the command. The men scattered in the trackside woods, knowing their likely fate if captured in civilian clothes. Andrews put the engine in reverse and followed his men into the woods. The General labored slowly south until the Texas' engineer saw it in time to slow down, couple on and set his brake, bringing the chase to an end.

Andrews was the first to meet the fate of spies, hanged in Atlanta on June 7, 1862, at the intersection of today's Juniper and Third Streets. Conductor William Fuller was among the witnesses. According to some accounts—not all—when Andrews fell through the trap, his feet just barely hit the ground, unfortunately prolonging his life. Someone frantically shoveled away earth from beneath his feet as he strangled. Seven others died on better gallows a few days later.[32]

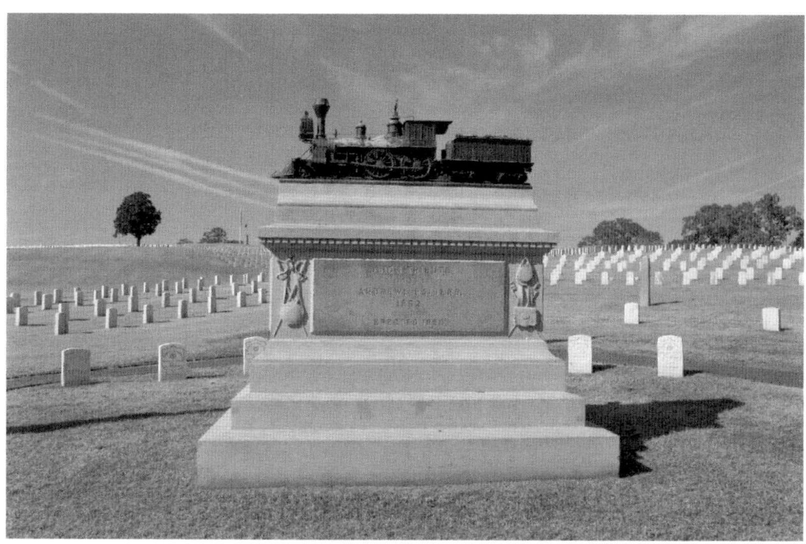

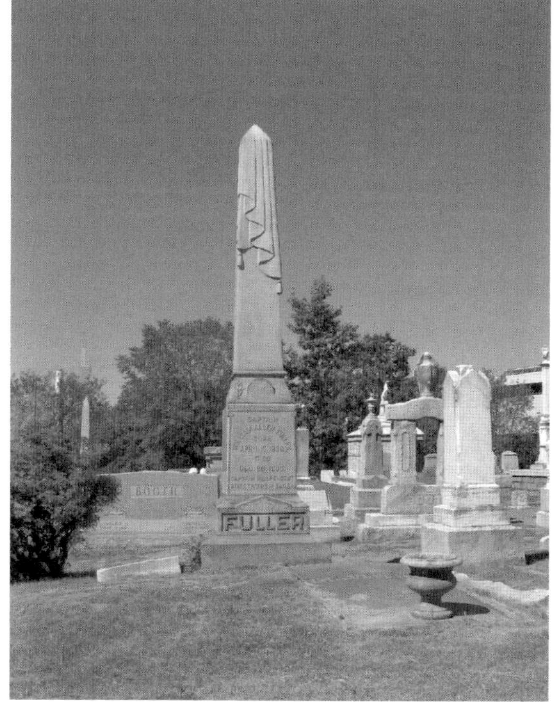

Above: The monument for the Andrews Raiders, established by the State of Ohio in 1891, in the Chattanooga National Cemetery. Surmounting the memorial is a bronze replica of the locomotive General. The General was built in 1855 by Rogers, Ketchum, and Grosvenor Locomotive Works in Paterson, New Jersey. Since 1972, it has been displayed at the Southern Museum of Civil War and Locomotive History in Kennesaw, Georgia. *Bob Price, photographer.*

Right: The grave of William A. Fuller (1838–1905). Oakland Cemetery is a pantheon of great figures in Atlanta's history. The grave of William A. Fuller is among the most visible and venerated. The Andrews Raiders could not have had a more dangerous opponent than Fuller. Fuller pursued them from Big Shanty to just past Ringgold and saw Andrews hang on June 7, 1862. *Bob Price, photographer.*

The others met varying fates. The two men who had missed the train at Big Shanty joined Confederate units. The rest were captured within two weeks. Counting Andrews, eight were hanged and six were exchanged. Nineteen of the survivors received the first Medals of Honor.

The W&A had successfully defended itself and its northern terminal. It was equipped by its nature to do so. Already by the time of the Civil War, railroads had become more than corporate entities and tracks linking stations. They operated within a precise schedule, an idea unknown elsewhere in the country. Thanks to bridge-building engineers and the builders of locomotives, they had a massive physical presence unmatched by anything else in the country. They operated at sustained speeds never attained before in human history. Personnel—railroaders—knew their schedules, their equipment, and where they were on the railroad at all times. The W&A had developed a personality apart from the ledger books. On this occasion, W&A railroaders reacted vigorously to the invasion of their railroad's world. In saving itself, the W&A served its owner, the state of Georgia, and its country well.

But the defense of the Confederate west continued to crumble. Beauregard's Army of Tennessee evacuated Corinth on May 30 and fell back to Tupelo. It soon had a new commander, General Braxton Bragg.

Memphis fell to the Union on June 6, the day before Andrews was hanged. On the day of the hanging, General Mitchel shelled Chattanooga, doing little damage but making headlines in Atlanta.[33] Mitchel soon withdrew, but later in the month, Buell's Army of the Ohio, thirty-five thousand men, began moving south. Fortunately for the Confederates, he depended "on the longest rail line of communication that any Federal commander had relied on since the War began. At least three hundred miles of line stretched southward from Louisville toward his most advanced position."[34]

Confederate cavalry raids broke his rail line of supply again and again, but by July 24, Buell had the Nashville & Chattanooga line in service as far as Stevenson, Alabama, less than fifty miles west of Chattanooga.[35]

With no Confederate force nearer to Chattanooga than E. Kirby Smith's small force at Knoxville, General Bragg understood Chattanooga's peril. "No greater disaster could befall the Confederacy than the loss of Chattanooga," he wrote.[36]

But the question was, could he reach Chattanooga before Buell? Bragg moved his army from Tupelo to Chattanooga by rail. Beginning with a single division on July 27, he moved his infantry by way of Meridian,

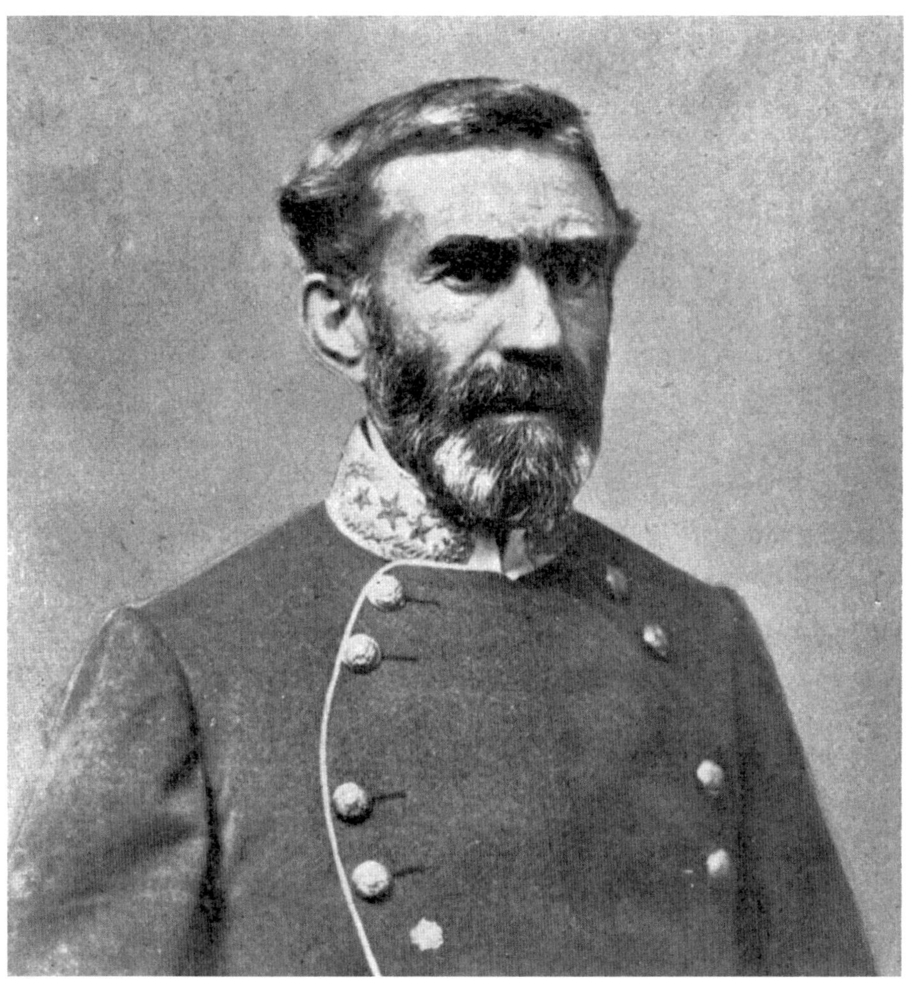

General Braxton Bragg (1817–1876). Bragg invaded Kentucky from Chattanooga in 1862 but was forced to evacuate Chattanooga on September 8, 1863. Despite his great victory at Chickamauga on September 19–20, 1863, he was unable to retake the northern terminal of the W&A. *From* The Photographic History of the Civil War in Ten Volumes, Semi-Centennial Memorial Edition, *Francis T. Miller, Editor-in-Chief, New York, The Review of Reviews Co., 1911.*

Mobile, Montgomery, and Atlanta—over six different railroads of at least two different gauges and including steamers to cross Mobile Bay. The last stretch was the easiest—138 miles over the W&A. The first division reached Chattanooga in six days. Bragg arrived on July 30, and "soon a procession of troop trains came curving around Missionary Ridge into town."[37]

In moving close to thirty thousand troops to Chattanooga, Bragg and the W&A set the stage for his own offensive into Kentucky. "For the time being, the whole complexion of the war in the west changed in favor of the South."[38]

Chapter 3

Abel D. Streight and Nathan Bedford Forrest

In the summer of 1862, the 55th Indiana Volunteer Infantry was stationed in Decatur, Alabama. Colonel Abel D. Streight was in command. The regiment was part of General James A. Garfield's brigade of the Army of the Ohio.[39] The regiment had seen no action at Shiloh and very little around Corinth. Colonel Streight, a man of great energy and deep Republican convictions, hated inactivity and longed to strike a meaningful blow for the Union.

He was born in Wheeler, New York, in Steuben County, in 1829. His father was a well-to-do farmer, but Abel had no interest in farming. Instead, he took up carpentry and soon went into the lumber business. He married Lovina McCarty, also from Steuben County, in 1849. The couple moved west in 1857, first to Cincinnati and then to Indianapolis. There he went into the publishing business.[40]

He took a keen interest in national politics. In 1856, he campaigned for John C. Frémont. He had nothing but contempt for President Buchanan and Senator Stephen A. Douglas. He saw them as weak and irresolute, unable or unwilling to stand up to the Southern states and their threat of secession. In 1860, he strongly supported Abraham Lincoln. In that year, he set forth his political principles in a tract of about one hundred pages, *The Crisis of Eighteen Hundred and Sixty-One in the Government of the United States: Its Cause, and How It Should Be Met.*

Secession, he wrote, was "our nation's calamity," brought on by the "mobocracy" of the South. He blamed Douglas and Buchanan for their vain and misguided attempts to appease the South. He was not concerned

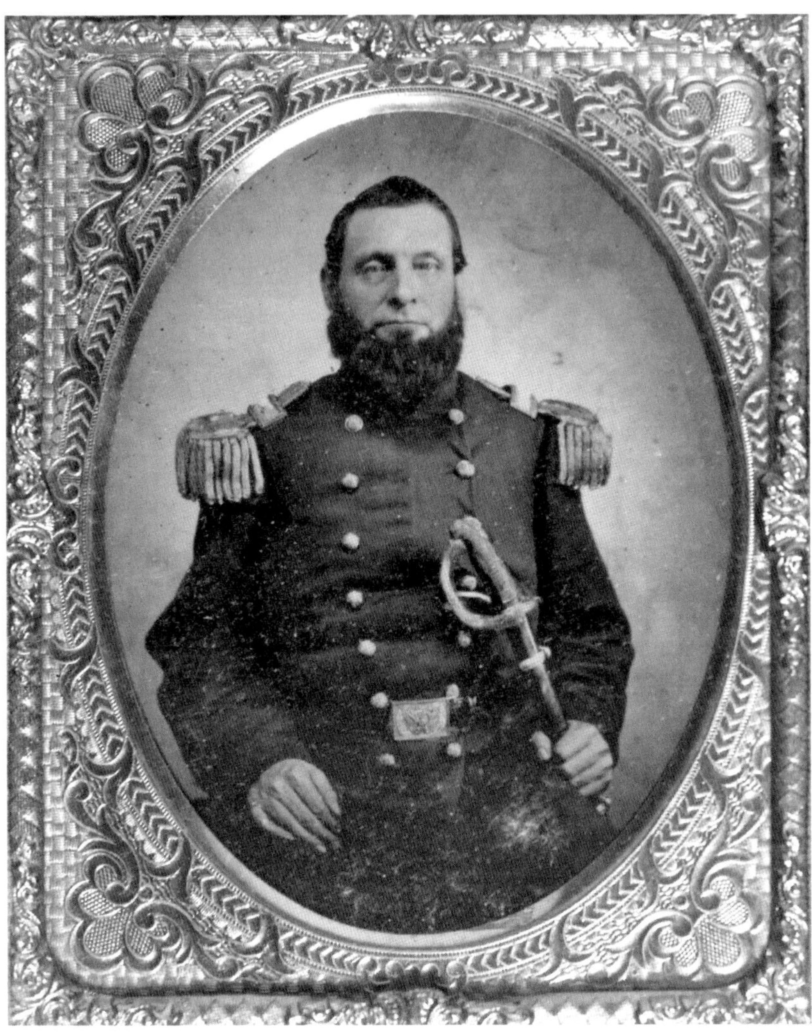

Colonel Abel D. Streight (1828–1892). Streight's devotion to the Union fueled his desire to carry the War behind Confederate lines. His opponent, Forrest, matched his determination and drive to force him to surrender. Streight was sent to Libby Prison in Richmond. He escaped, not surprisingly, to serve again. *Courtesy Indiana State Historical Society (PO332), Indianapolis, Indiana.*

about slavery. "I am not one of those who think that the question of slavery is the great and only cause of our present troubles…far from it." The true cause was the unprovoked, unwarranted, and indefensible challenge to Federal authority in matters of "taxes, duties, imposts, and excises"—the Federal revenue.

The Southern states were no longer sovereign in any real sense, he argued. He conceded them the moral right to secede but only in the case of severe and continual oppression. There was no such justification. If they proceeded with disunion, let it come to "one grand battle." So be it. "War would be to our political system, what the thunderstorm is to the atmosphere…inspiring new life, vigor, and purity…the mad project of disunion" must be purged. Fear that war would be worse for the country than secession was foolish, he wrote.[11]

Also in 1860, Streight asked his friend, Indiana's governor Oliver Perry Morton, for a letter of introduction to President-elect Lincoln. Lincoln was still in Springfield, though he would leave soon for Washington. Perry obliged, and Streight went to Lincoln's house in Springfield. He found Lincoln besieged by office seekers. He gave his letter to "a young colored man," along with his own note saying that he was *not* seeking office. Lincoln soon sent for him; Streight said they talked for two hours. Streight said he urged Lincoln to keep the Republican Party's core intact by not compromising in any way with the South. The president then said, "though not for publication," that he did not "understand that the President had any discretion as to whether he would enforce the laws or not, provided the people furnish the means."[12]

Back in Indianapolis, on September 4, Streight got what he wanted most: not a political appointment from the president but an officer's commission from his governor. He was posted as colonel in the 51st Indiana Volunteer Infantry Regiment. In the summer of 1862, the regiment was at Decatur, with Streight longing for action.

The Union occupation of North Alabama, which Mitchel had initiated in April, was now in full force. Buell had reached Huntsville in early June, aiming at Chattanooga.[13] That month, Streight saw an opportunity to defeat "the mad project of disunion": he would go to the aid of Alabama Unionists—Tories to the Confederates. They became his particular passion. Helping them and enlisting their support was the best way he knew to act on his interpretation of the Constitution, to weaken the Confederacy from within.

Alabama was not as deeply or evenly divided as Tennessee, but there was a marked split in political opinion between the Tennessee River Valley counties and the hill country counties from twenty to forty miles south of the river. The Valley counties, where slavery was widespread, were solidly Confederate, but "the up-country people were politically closer to East Tennesseans than they were to most Alabamians."[14]

Alabama Unionists were, generally speaking, "cooperationists" during the Secession Crisis and passive in the first year of the War. But with the passage in April 1862 of the Confederate Conscription Act, "Union sympathizers in northeast Alabama took to the hills and caves."[45] Clashes with "conscription cavalry" became more and more numerous, alarming Confederate authorities in Montgomery. But North Alabama, though divided, was not Unionist. Streight may have overestimated the strength of Unionism in Alabama. He saw it as a Southern vindication of his own beliefs. He took up their cause as his own, "to give them protection and a chance to defend the flag of their country."

In Decatur, Unionists from the hill country told him that he would find willing recruits south of the Tennessee River, if he could bring them safely into Union lines. In July, he asked Buell for orders to lead a small force from Decatur south to Davis' Gap, one of the passes through the Sand Mountain plateau, twenty-five miles south. Buell's chief of staff sent him permission to go but restricted his expedition to three days and warned him "to see that they are not playing a trick to draw you out." Streight left Decatur on July 12 with three companies of the 51st Indiana and 16 men from the 1st Ohio Cavalry under Captain R.C. Writer. But the two officers could not coordinate their movements—Streight accused Writer of "direct disobedience."[46] A body of conscript cavalry attacked the Ohioans, routing them in a complete surprise. Writer was badly wounded and lost his sword. The cavalrymen returned to Decatur ahead of Streight. Still, Streight claimed that he brought out 150 volunteers. With more time and men, he could have brought out an entire regiment. But he had to wait for another opportunity to strike a blow for the Union.

On July 13, 1862, the day after Streight marched three companies of infantry out of Decatur, heading for Sand Mountain, Brigadier General Nathan Bedford Forrest led about 1,400 cavalrymen into Murfreesboro, Tennessee, and captured the entire Union garrison. It was his forty-first birthday.

Like Abel Streight, Nathan Bedford Forrest was raised on a farm, and like Streight, he turned away from farming. Both men moved west; both settled in large, but very different, cities; and both were successful businessmen in very different businesses. Both were favored by the governors of their states. There the similarity between the two men ends.

The title of Brian Wills' biography of Forrest, *Battle from the Start*, is well chosen. Forrest was a product of the frontier. Born in 1821 near Chapel Hill,

Tennessee, in Bedford County, the young Forrest's first battle was against frontier poverty. His father died early; by the time Bedford was seventeen, he was the head of his family—his mother and nine siblings. He went west, first to Tippah County, Mississippi; then to Hernando, twenty miles from Memphis; and finally to Memphis. He had little time for education and was no stranger to violence. He survived encounters with wild animals and two gunfights in Hernando, where he was constable and coroner. By 1845, he owned three slaves.

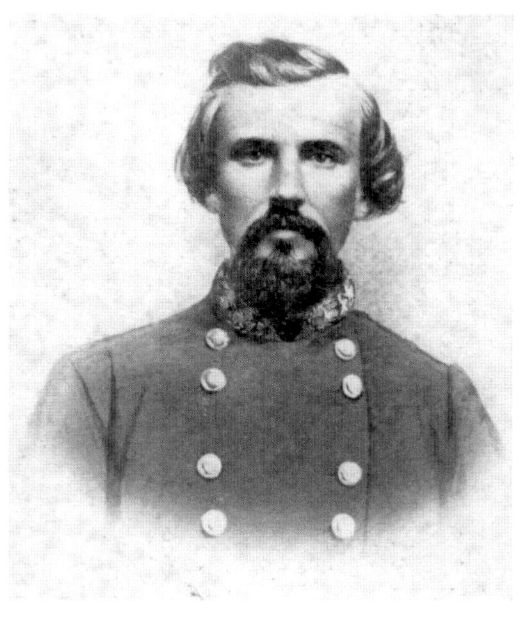

Brigadier General Nathan Bedford Forrest (1821–1877). This photograph of Forrest as brigadier general, with his uniform retouched by hand, was taken in 1862. He ended the War as lieutenant-general. *Alabama Department of Archives and History, Montgomery, Alabama.*

He prospered even more in Memphis, in real estate and the slave trade. By 1860, he owned thirty-six slaves and nearly 3,500 acres in Coahoma County, Mississippi. The census of 1860 listed his occupation as planter. He was also an alderman in Memphis. He was not a secessionist. By 1860–61, "change was something Bedford neither needed or wanted."[17]

Still, he followed his state out of the Union. He enlisted in a cavalry company, but Governor Isham Harris soon commissioned him lieutenant colonel in a regiment Forrest would raise himself. In February 1862, rather than follow his craven superiors in surrendering Fort Donelson, he led his men out of the fort the night before the surrender. "Forrest led his troops to safety, under conditions which would have broken the will of any ordinary man as he was to do on many occasions in the years that followed."[18] Knowing that Nashville could not be held after Fort Donelson fell, he took his command there and brought some order out of the near anarchy of evacuation, saving valuable supplies.

Forrest commanded a brigade at Shiloh, both in Johnston's attack on April 6 and in the rear guard action at Fallen Timbers on April 7. In that fight, he suffered a severe wound, shot in the side, the ball lodging next to his spine. Even so, he stayed in the saddle, scooping up a Federal soldier as he rode out of danger—a human shield until he was out of range, when he pushed him off.

By June 1862, when Colonel Streight was chafing for some kind of action in North Alabama, Forrest was a brigadier general, a veteran of hard fighting in Kentucky and Tennessee. He was known as a hard and almost always victorious fighter who led his men by personal example. It was the Murfreesboro raid that prompted Forrest's proverbial explanation of his military prowess: "I just took the shortcut and got there first with the most men."[49] In December, during Grant's first Vicksburg campaign, he broke Grant's line of railroad supply at Jackson, Tennessee. When General Earl Van Dorn, soon to be Forrest's superior, destroyed Grant's supply depot at Holly Springs, the two cavalry commanders effectively saved Vicksburg until the following summer.

Forrest's reputation had not yet reached mythic proportions, but he was a formidable combat officer and an impressive figure. Chaplain W.H. Whitsitt rode with Forrest in 1863, and he described him as "a man of remarkable appearance, over six feet tall, somewhat muscular in build, powerful and graceful, giving an appearance of solidity and completeness; while neatly dressed and groomed, he apparently took no thought of dress or accouterments and was altogether devoid of personal vanity."[50]

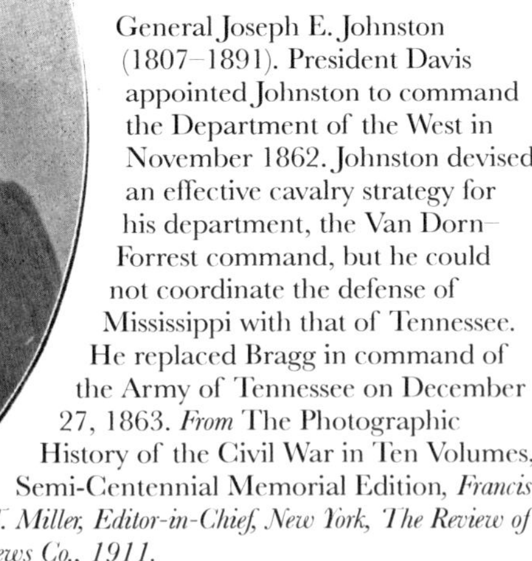

General Joseph E. Johnston (1807–1891). President Davis appointed Johnston to command the Department of the West in November 1862. Johnston devised an effective cavalry strategy for his department, the Van Dorn–Forrest command, but he could not coordinate the defense of Mississippi with that of Tennessee. He replaced Bragg in command of the Army of Tennessee on December 27, 1863. *From* The Photographic History of the Civil War in Ten Volumes, Semi-Centennial Memorial Edition, *Francis T. Miller, Editor-in-Chief, New York, The Review of Reviews Co., 1911.*

The last months of 1862 brought great changes to Confederate strategy in the West. After the great disappointments and defeats in the fall—Bragg's withdrawal from Kentucky, the bloody battles of Iuka and Corinth, the beginning of Grant's offensive aimed at Vicksburg—President Jefferson Davis and Secretary of War James Seddon put Confederate strategy in the West on new footing. Deeply worried about Mississippi (Vicksburg) and Tennessee (Chattanooga), President Davis appointed General Joseph E. Johnston to "theater" command in the West. Without a field command himself, Johnston, from his headquarters in Chattanooga, was to coordinate the movements of both Bragg's Army of Tennessee and General John C. Pemberton's Army of Mississippi. Johnston arrived in Chattanooga on December 4.

Before Johnston could act, there was good news, first from Forrest and Van Dorn, and then, on the last day of the year, from Bragg. Bragg reported a great victory over General William R. Rosecrans, Buell's successor, at Murfreesboro. "We occupy the whole field and shall follow him. God has granted us a Happy New Year."[51]

But the bitter reality soon dawned; Bragg had not triumphed, and he soon fell back to Tullahoma. With Rosecrans in a position to move on Chattanooga, Johnston faced a strategic crisis. He had no reinforcements for Bragg.[52] His first response was sound. He wrote to President Davis on January 1, "I wish to organize a cavalry

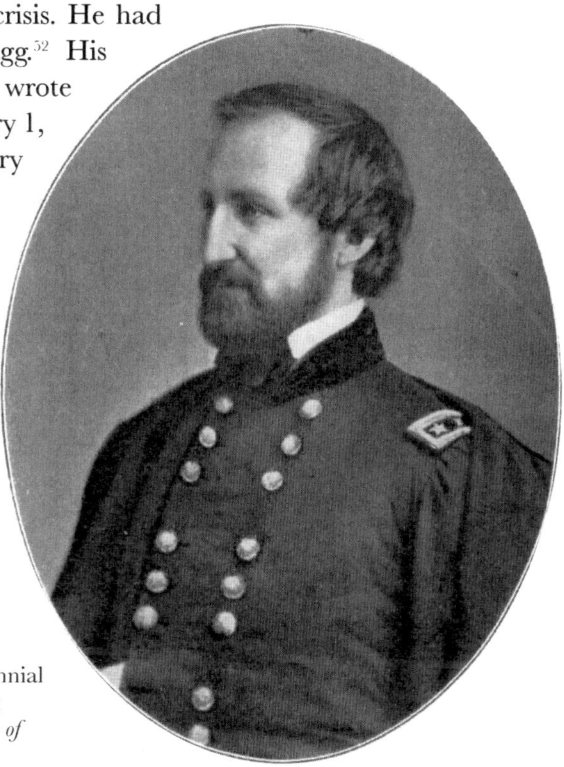

General William Rosecrans (1819–1898). Rosecrans succeeded Buell as commander of the Army of the Cumberland (previously the Army of the Ohio) in October 1862. After his victory at the Battle of Murfreesboro, President Lincoln prodded Rosecrans into "counter-raids." Rosecrans then authorized the Streight Raid. *From* The Photographic History of the Civil War in Ten Volumes, Semi-Centennial Memorial Edition, *Francis T. Miller, Editor-in-Chief, New York, The Review of Reviews Co., 1911.*

expedition in the two departments. Please assign General Van Dorn to the same cavalry with instructions to report to me."[53] On January 17, he told President Davis, "I am preparing to send about 6,000 cavalry under Van Dorn to Bragg's aid to operate on the enemy's communications."[54]

Johnston ordered Van Dorn to bring two brigades from Mississippi to Columbia and Spring Hill, Tennessee, on Bragg's left. Forrest would join him with his brigade from Bragg's army to make up a force of about 6,300 men "present and effective," to disrupt communications between Grant and Rosecrans and threaten the lines of supply of both.[55]

Once again, however, bitter reality dawned. As Johnston explained to a nervous Pemberton in March, "Van Dorn's cavalry is absolutely necessary to enable General Bragg to hold the best part of the country from which he draws his supplies."[56] In other words, Johnston learned that the force he had assembled to disrupt the communications and lines of supply of two Federal armies was going to have to hold its ground in order to protect Bragg's line of supply and communication.

South of Nashville, in what has been described as a "fencing match," the Confederates inflicted stinging defeats on Union forces at Thompson's Station (March 5) and Brentwood (March 25). Forrest displayed the same qualities of leadership and prowess that he had shown in 1861–62. His reputation began to grow into mythic proportions. For example, one of the first Forrest horse stories comes from Thompson's Station. Forrest was riding his favorite horse, Roderick, a chestnut. According to the story, Roderick was wounded three times and Forrest sent him back, hoping to save his life. But before anyone could tend to him, Roderick broke free and ran back to where he had last seen his master. He was wounded again, this time fatally. He is buried near where he fell, on the grounds of today's Roderick Place.[57]

In the clash at Brentwood, Sergeant J.G. Witherspoon of the 4th Tennessee described an incident that is "pure Forrest"—i.e., typical of his battlefield processes and personality. Witherspoon's regiment was advancing, slowly, on Federal troops firing from behind a stone wall. Then,

> *General Forrest came charging up the pike, cursing a blue streak as he came. He had a considerable force, seven or eight hundred men. (I learned afterward that in coming up the pike he had gathered a conglomerated medley of men of different commands that had been stampeded.) He had a flag in his hand, which he waved over his head. As he came up I heard him say, "Fall in! every damned one of you!". I presume that he thought we had stampeded too. We fell in, of course. We couldn't have stayed out if*

we had wanted to... We charged up the pike like the Old Scratch was after us. When we got within good long range of their muskets, which we could see glistening from behind the stone fences, two or three to one of us, and I began to think, "Old man, I wonder if you are going to charge those fences in the shape we are in"—for we were going then in column of fours—he reined up his horse and commanded "Halt!" Turning his horse he looked back down the line, then said coolly as if he were simply on his way to church, "Boys, I'll be damned if it will do to charge like that!"

Forrest ordered his men to swing to the Union right. After they cleared it, the cavalrymen dismounted and drove the Federals back about two miles. "We were bothered with them no more that day."[58]

Despite Forrest and Van Dorn's victories, both of Johnston's field commanders were worried. Pemberton was nervous about his shortage of cavalry because Van Dorn had been sent to Tennessee. Bragg was worried about a shortage of almost everything except cavalry. Like most generals, Bragg felt logistically short-changed. He fought hard to get what he believed he needed to maintain his army's subsistence, equipment, and firepower. "Despite substantial evidence that [his] men were well fed throughout the spring of 1863, Bragg continued to insist that there was a severe shortage of meat," among other necessary supplies.[59] As he pleaded his case, the correspondence between Bragg, Secretary of War Seddon, Johnston, and Commissary General Lucious K. Northrup became heated. At the same time, Bragg sought to stop his men from foraging on farms of loyal citizens. Abhorring any breach of discipline, he warned his "commanders to institute rigid scrutiny and to use all means in their power to suppress the evil," including banishing to an infantry regiment any cavalrymen caught in the act.[60] He complained bitterly about commissary agents.

There were ample stores on hand in Atlanta, and the W&A was there to move supplies to Chattanooga. Johnston had placed Chattanooga under Bragg's orders, but the results were far from ideal. The problem with supplies did not lie in Chattanooga. It lay in what Larry Daniel, historian of the Army of Tennessee, has called a "logistical inequity": W&A trains rolled north from Atlanta, but many trains kept rolling through Chattanooga or Dalton, bound for Virginia. Early in February, Northrup had decreed that "the army in Virginia is in a critical need for subsistence and the supplies… at Atlanta and in North Georgia are needed for it and are held for it alone."[61]

On balance, it seems that Bragg's army was reasonably well supplied. He could not, however, afford to lose his sources of supply in Tennessee or the line of the W&A for any significant length of time. When ordnance supplies were slow to come north, Bragg lost patience with the W&A and threatened to seize it and operate it himself. An alarmed and angry Governor Brown appealed to the president, who defused the crisis. Brown then promised to see to it that more trains went through to Chattanooga to be unloaded there rather than in Virginia. The results are not clear.[62] Commissary officers in Atlanta did, on occasion, dispatch bacon to Bragg on their own initiative. Clearly, the Army of Tennessee could not do without the W&A. The W&A was vital to two great Rebel armies.[63]

Chapter 4

Abraham Lincoln: "We Should Organize Forces and Make Counter Raids"

On February 17, 1863, President Lincoln wrote to General Rosecrans in Murfreesboro. Six weeks had passed since Rosecrans' victory in the Battle of Murfreesboro (Stone's River). Rosecrans' Army of the Cumberland, formerly the Army of the Ohio, had not moved since. Wanting movement of some kind, Lincoln wrote, "In no other way does the enemy give us so much trouble at so little expense to himself as by the raids of rapidly moving small bodies of troops…I think we should organize forces and make counter raids…It would trouble them more to repair railroads and bridges than it does us."

Because Rosecrans had been pleading a shortage of horses, Lincoln promised him "horses, arms, and other appointments."[64]

A few weeks later on March 5, a future president, Rosecrans' chief of staff James A. Garfield, received a letter from Abel Streight. Streight wanted to organize a rapidly moving small body of troops "for the purpose of penetrating the interior of the south." He asked Garfield to suggest it to Rosecrans, saying, "I could do them more harm and our cause more good in a three-month campaign than I can, situated as I have been during the last year, in a whole lifetime."[65]

Garfield endorsed Streight's suggestion, and so did Rosecrans. Rosecrans ordered Garfield to organize such an expedition but forbade him from leading it himself.[66]

As Garfield and Streight began to work out a definite plan and mission, the Union high command got involved, in fast widening circles.[67] Rosecrans believed that whatever Streight's mission became, his Army of the Cumberland force needed support from General Grenville Dodge's division of the Army of the Tennessee's XVI Corps at Corinth, Mississippi. Rosecrans approached Dodge directly, rather than through his superior, Major General Stephen Hurlbut, in Memphis. The planning then came to involve Hurlbut's superior, General Ulysses S. Grant. Hurlbut favored a simultaneous cavalry raid into Mississippi, the Grierson raid (April 17–May 2). On April 6, he wrote to Grant's headquarters to say, "The Streight-Dodge movement will… draw off those cavalry forces into Alabama and leave my field clear. The cavalry dash I desire to time so as to cooperate with what I suppose to be your plan, to land below Vicksburg."[68] Since Grant's objective in the spring was Vicksburg, Streight's proposal—a raid to cut the W&A—was part of a far larger plan to divert Confederate attention away from Grant.

On April 17, Colonel Benjamin Grierson left LaGrange, Tennessee, with 1,700 men, to draw away from Vicksburg what little cavalry Pemberton had. Hurlbut assured Grant that Streight's raid, still in planning, would hold Van Dorn's cavalry in Tennessee or Alabama.

The mission and plan for the Streight Raid became clear on April 8, 1863. In Special Field Orders No. 94, Garfield announced the creation of Streight's Independent Provisional Brigade as follows:

Colonel Abel D. Streight
Independent Provisional Brigade[69]
Approximately 1,700 men

3rd Ohio Infantry	Lieutenant Colonel Robert Lawson
51st Indiana Infantry	Lieutenant Colonel James W. Sheets
73rd Indiana Infantry	Colonel Gilbert Hathaway
80th Illinois Infantry	Lieutenant Colonel Andrew F. Rodgers
1st West Tennessee/Alabama (U.S.) Cavalry, Companies L, K	Captain David D. Smith
Battery unknown, (2) twelve-pounder mountain howitzers	Lieutenant J.W. Pavey

Confederate chaplain Whitsitt described the men making up Streight's brigade as "brave and formidable. They were select and seasoned infantry, from Indiana, Ohio, and Illinois…They were practiced and patient fighters."[70]

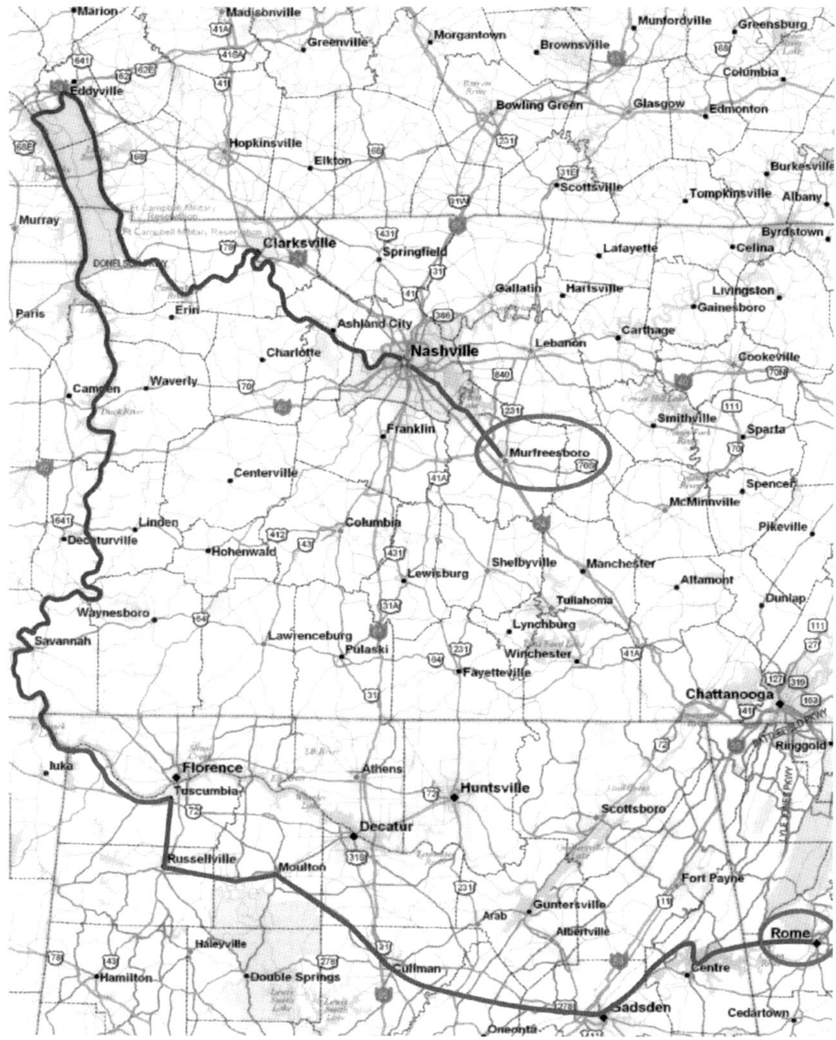

Route of the Streight Raid. The presence of the Van Dorn–Forrest cavalry force, south of Franklin, Tennessee, necessitated the immensely long and circuitous route Streight had to follow—down the Cumberland, then up the Tennessee to Eastport, Mississippi—in order to begin his raid. *Larry Johnson.*

Streight's orders were to move from Murfreesboro to Nashville, board transports there and head down the Cumberland River to Palmyra, Tennessee. There he was to disembark and march overland to Fort Henry on the Tennessee River, where the transports and Captain Alfred W. Ellett's Marine Brigade flotilla would re-join him to take him up the Tennessee River to "some good steamboat landing, debark, and join a force under Brigadier General Grenville M. Dodge."[71]

Streight was to meet Dodge but not become part of his force. Dodge's mission, set by Army of the Tennessee headquarters in Memphis, was to take Tuscumbia and then advance on Decatur, Alabama, pinning down Confederate forces long enough for Streight to get underway ahead of any belated pursuit. Dodge's force, 3,500 infantry and 1,500 cavalry, was far stronger than Confederate colonel Phillip D. Roddey's cavalry covering Tuscumbia. As Dodge advanced, the Marine Brigade would come upriver as far as Muscle Shoals to protect Dodge's rear from any Confederate force crossing the Tennessee River.[72] In other words, Dodge would be Streight's screen, behind which he was to "cut loose" and ride for Moulton, Alabama, on to Rome, Georgia, and then to the W&A between Kingston and Chattanooga. He was to "keep well mounted from the country through which you will pass." The expectation was that Alabama Unionists would help him. He was to ignore any "collateral or incidental schemes" and refrain from "pillage and marauding." He would have ample U.S. currency. His troops would wear full U.S. uniforms, unlike Andrews' men. But Garfield offered little hope of escape after Streight completed his mission, saying, "You may return by way of Northern Alabama or Northern Georgia. Should you be surrounded by rebel forces and your retreat cut off, defend yourself as long as possible and make the surrender of your command cost the enemy as many of their number as possible."[73]

The vast operation posed a challenge to the planners—coordinating the movements of troops from different commands over great distances. The challenge to the Confederates was even more severe. As the operation unfolded, "every major Confederate cavalry command between the Appalachians and the Mississippi River was engaged in trying to contain the hydra-headed tentacles launched by the Federals."[74]

Streight faced the greatest opportunity of his life: to carry the flag of the Union behind Confederate lines, destroy a vital railroad, and rally Unionists to the cause. It might become a triumphant procession across North Alabama to the mountains of north Georgia. But he was not a cavalryman. His experience with cavalry in North Alabama had not been good. His troops were mounted infantry. The Confederates could be expected to react with speed and power. It was important to get out ahead of whatever pursuit they might send. But, again, he could not move south from Nashville to meet Dodge at Corinth—a little less than 100 miles—because of the presence of Van Dorn and Forrest south of Franklin. His route to meet Dodge near

Tuscumbia, Alabama, was 350 miles long. Garfield saw no serious difficulty in the execution of the plan. "Colonel Streight will make himself heard from in the course of a week or so I now think," he commented to his wife.[75]

Mules

William Faulkner reared mules on his farm and knew them well. He included them in many of the most memorable scenes in his Yoknapatawpha novels. He said of them: "Father and mother he does not resemble, sons and daughters he will never have; vindictive and patient (it is a known fact that he will labor ten years willingly and patiently for you, for the privilege of kicking you once)."[76]

There was another serious problem: What were these mounted infantrymen going to ride? Rosecrans had never stopped complaining that he lacked enough horses for his cavalry. The War Department and Quartermaster General Meigs vehemently disagreed. It was a standoff. The result for Streight, he reported, was a decision—whose, he did not say—to mount his men on mules. "I was instructed to draw about half the number of mules necessary to mount my command at Nashville and to seize in the country through which I passed the remaining number of animals to mount the balance."[77]

Mules are the product of union between mares and donkeys. From the mare they get the shape of their neck and croup and their bay or brown coats. The short mane, long ears, thin legs, small hooves, and bray come from the donkey. They work hard and long on little forage. They are proverbially stubborn and very sure-footed. They were best suited for hauling wagons and bearing packs. They did the best they could and, like horses, suffered terribly. But they were not the best choice for Streight's infantrymen.[78] (Streight's men would always fight dismounted.)[79]

The brigade left Nashville on April 10 in eight transports, headed down the Cumberland for Palmyra. They disembarked there on April 11 for the trek to Fort Henry. The animals were frightened and miserable. It was only at Palmyra that Streight discovered that Rosecrans had given him "nothing but poor, wild, and unbroken colts," many sick with horse distemper. What Streight called "horse distemper," many of his men familiar with horse and mules might have called "tempers" or "strangles." Whatever it was called, this equine respiratory ailment brings horrible symptoms—discharge from the nostrils and eyes, high temperature, painful cough, and swollen lymph nodes. It is debilitating, likely fatal, and highly contagious.[80] Nearly fifty mules were terribly ill and had to be left behind at Palmyra. In the morning, "such of them as could be rode at all were so unmanageable that it took us all day and a part of the next to catch and break them before we could set out across the country."[81] Once underway, Streight sent out foragers to gather more, or as one soldier, Stanton Brumfield, wrote, "We went to stealing mules and horses."[82] Brumfield went on to say, "Some of the mules would get contrary and would not go and then there would be some would throw the rider or lay down with him very often in the middle of the creek."[83]

The brigade left Palmyra on April 13. With nearly five hundred men still on foot, it reached Fort Henry on April 15. On the same day, Dodge's cavalry led his force out of Corinth, heading for Tuscumbia.

When Streight reached Fort Henry, he was disappointed to find no waiting transports. The vessels had picked up rations for Dodge's force and were still en route up the Tennessee. They arrived near midnight on April 15, together with the vessels carrying Ellett's Marine Brigade. Loading up the Provisional Brigade and its animals consumed more time on the sixteenth. Then, the river pilots balked at leaving Eastport before the morning of the seventeenth.[84] They didn't want to go upriver at night.

The delays were beginning to mount up. Streight was not subject to such a precise timetable as Andrews had been, but delays in reaching Dodge could wear away at Dodge's intention of keeping his force out in front as a fighting screen. He may have already been eyeing the rich, fertile, undefended Tennessee River Valley plantation country.

The flotilla had grown in size by the time it was finally underway. Ellett's Marine Brigade—five transports, two gunboats, and a ram—joined Streight's eight transports. Sebastian Brumfield described the voyage in his letter to his wife, Mary: "We are getting way down sout [*sic*] in Dixie in the rear of old Bragg. The state of Mississippi is on the right of us and we will soon be in Alabama. I expect we are coming down here to raise old Ned, but I am afraid if we are not careful they will raise old Ned with us."[85]

From Savannah on April 18, Streight wired Dodge that he expected to be at Eastport the next day and would come up to see him. Once ashore, he left immediately for Dodge's headquarters, twelve miles north at Great Bear Creek. He left Colonel Robert Lawson in command to supervise the unloading.

Although the only Confederates facing Dodge were Colonel Phillip Roddey's outnumbered regiments, Dodge moved with extreme caution.

However, his men did range far from the road. One infantryman noted in his diary that they "burned everything within four miles of the road on either side."[86]

District of North Alabama
Colonel Phillip D. Roddey[87]

4th Alabama Cavalry	Colonel W.A. Johnson
53rd Alabama Cavalry	Colonel M.W. Hannon
Julian's Alabama Cavalry Battalion	Major William R. Julian
Baxter's Alabama Partisan Cavalry Battalion	Captain G.L. Baxter
Ferrell's Georgia Light Artillery (Accompanied Forrest from Courtland to Cedar Bluff; only two guns were present at Cedar Bluff)	Captain C.B. Ferrell

Although Dodge had gone well beyond Great Bear Creek, by the time Streight reached him, he had fallen back, calling for reinforcements. Dodge told Streight that he expected to advance again on April 22 or 23. Streight should keep to the rear before cutting loose.

Streight then returned to Eastport, reaching the landing at about midnight. Appalling news awaited him. The mules had been brought ashore onto the bluff overlooking the river, where they had been penned in some fashion. But there had been a stampede. According to local lore, two of Roddey's scouts had already discovered the enemy's presence. They heard the brays of hundreds of mules and crept close to stampede them. They threw in sacks of hornets' nests and fired pistols into the air. The mules, on land for the first time in eleven days, must have been on a hair trigger of anger and fear. They bolted, careened down the bluff away from the river, and went downhill into a deep creek. Many were stung to death, while others drowned. "Daylight revealed to me," Streight wrote, "that nearly four hundred of our best animals were gone." It took a day and a half to round up about half of them. In a dispatch to Garfield, Streight implied that Colonel Lawson was to blame for not preventing the stampede.[88]

It's hard to imagine a more inauspicious beginning to a military operation. Streight had been on the move since April 7. He would not leave Eastport until the twenty-first, and the raid had not even begun. His men still were not all mounted. And if Roddey's scouts had indeed stampeded the mules, some Confederates knew something was up. But Abel Streight was not discouraged. He may have thought that surely the worst was over: the brigade had its mission and was moving on. On the afternoon of April 21, the brigade left Eastport to meet Dodge's command at Buzzard Roost, about thirty miles west of Tuscumbia. It rained heavily, and the guides lost their way. Everyone had a miserable night.[89] The following day boded well—the command was now close to becoming an independent raiding force. That day, Streight welcomed the arrival of his de facto second-in-command and close friend, Colonel Gilbert Hathaway. He took command of the 73rd Indiana.[90]

On April 23, Streight told his men where they were going and why. He explained "the perilous undertaking upon which we had started. That we would have to penetrate hundreds of miles into the enemy's country, would be surrounded by a wily foe for weeks, and if successful, we would have to subsist upon the country for rations."[91]

As Dodge moved into Tuscumbia, Streight made his final preparations. He culled his ranks for those too sick to go on, leaving them with Dodge. Dodge, in turn, gave him some mules, rations, and six wagons. He also gave him some important news: Forrest had crossed the Tennessee River and was in the vicinity of Town Creek (east of Tuscumbia). Dodge assured Streight, however, that he would "advance as far as Courtland on the Decatur Road, and if possible drive the enemy in that direction, but if they turned toward Moulton [Streight's intended first destination], our cavalry under General Dodge was to be kept in pursuit. With this understanding, I moved from Tuscumbia on the night of the 26th inst. in the direction of Moulton…with three hundred men still on foot."[92] He sent a last dispatch to Garfield: he hoped to have a two- or three-day lead on any pursuit, but if he was pushed too hard, "I will turn upon them and give them battle in the mountains."[93] Battle in the mountains would mean hard fighting, because Forrest would pursue "like a wolf coming down on a fold."[94] (See map on page 48.)

Chapter 5

"Cutting Loose" and Staying "Clost on Them"

Forrest was already moving. On April 23, orders came to him at Spring Hill from Bragg. He was to cross the Tennessee River and reinforce Roddey.[95]

District of North Alabama
Brigadier General Nathan Bedford Forrest's Brigade[96]
Approximately 1,600 men

4th Tennessee Cavalry	Lieutenant Colonel W.S. McLemore
8th (13th) Tennessee Cavalry	Colonel George C. Dibrell
9th Tennessee Cavalry	Colonel Jacob Biffle
10th Tennessee Cavalry	Colonel Wiliam E. DeMoss
11th Tennessee Cavalry	Colonel James H. Edmondson
Scouts	Captain William Forrest
Escort	Captain John C. Jackson (Montgomery Little was killed at Thompson's Station on March 5, 1863)
Morton's battery—Sent to Decatur after the skirmish at Town Creek, except for two rifled guns under Lieutenant Colonel Willis Gould, which went with Forrest. Streight captured them at Day's Gap. Forrest recaptured them, spiked, at Hog Mountain.	Captain John W. Morton

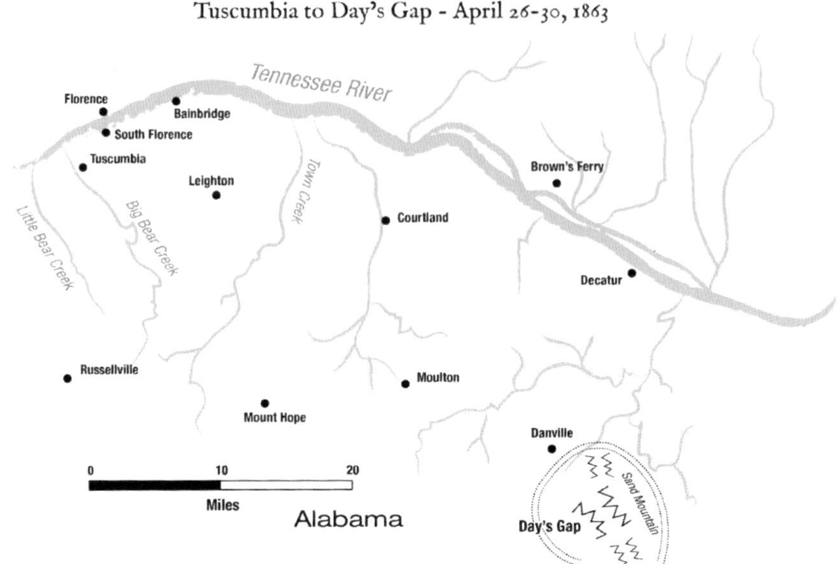

Forrest immediately ordered Edmondson's 4th Tennessee to cross the river at Bainbridge that night. The rest of the command left early the next morning to cross at Brown's Ferry. Making forty miles a day in heavy rain, Forrest arrived there on the night of April 26. On the morning of the twenty-seventh, he joined Roddey, skirmishing with Dodge from Leighton to Town Creek.

Forrest was always more than a hard rider and fighter. Until he could be certain beyond any doubt of the enemy's intentions, he divided and reunited his force in order to cover as many contingencies as he safely could. On the twenty-seventh, before crossing at Brown's Ferry, he sent the 8th (and possibly the 10th) Tennessee, under Colonel George C. Dibrell, with a section of Captain John Morton's battery, to Florence, Alabama, to threaten crossing behind Dodge. He moved on with the rest of the command—about 1,600 men—to join Roddey near Courtland.[97]

Streight broke away for Moulton late on April 26. He hoped to arrive there, forty miles away, the next night. But slowed by rain and many men still on foot, he had to halt at Mount Hope and wait there nearly twelve hours while his command came up.[98] He made camp near present-day Rock Springs Presbyterian Church. While Streight waited, some soldiers slipped away to plunder the nearby Templeton Plantation House.[99]

Dodge, meanwhile, engaged Forrest and Roddey in a heavy skirmish at Town Creek on April 28. He informed Streight by courier at Mount Hope that "he [Dodge] had driven the enemy and that I [by which he meant Streight] should push on." Also, crucially, Dodge informed Streight that he now considered his mission accomplished and was returning to Tuscumbia and Corinth.[100] He described his decision (on the day Streight surrendered): "Having accomplished my mission…I fell back to Tuscumbia…destroying 60 flat boats and ferries on the Tennessee River, thereby preventing Van Dorn in his move, from crossing to my rear."[101]

But Dodge had not driven the Confederates to Courtland or Decatur. He had been away from Corinth since the fifteenth and may have been concerned about his line of retreat. The Marine Brigade had returned to Eastport, while at Florence, Debrell was spreading the false word that Van Dorn's whole command was about to cross the Tennessee River.[102] Van Dorn was not coming, but as Warren Grabau wrote, "The terrible Forrest had been ordered to disengage before Streight was underway."[103]

It was during the fighting at Town Creek that Forrest first learned that here was a large Federal cavalry force farther south, perhaps aiming at his flank or rear. One of Roddey's scouts, James Mhoon, had seen what he estimated to be two thousand Federal cavalry heading for Mount Hope and moving on for Moulton.[104]

After listening to Mhoon and one other scout, Forrest pulled back from Town Creek to Courtland, sixteen miles from Moulton, to see what more he could learn: Was he fighting the wrong force? Had he been taken in by a screen? What was the Yankee force the scouts had seen? Where was it going? And what about Dodge? His force was clearly larger than the mysterious cavalry to the south. Was it the greater danger?

The fact was, the two Federal commands were moving in two different directions. Dodge, leaving one mission uncompleted, was now on a new mission: retreating to Tuscumbia and Corinth but bringing "total war" to the Tennessee Valley on his way. John McKee, of the 2nd Iowa, in Dodge's command, noted in his diary, "We burned all the plantation houses except one or two, burned LaGrange College…and there was none less than 105 houses burned."[105] Captain James Dinkins wrote that flames consumed everything "from the mountains to the river, from Town Creek to Tuscumbia…burning fields, granaries, meat houses, stables, and mansions."[106]

But Forrest was not following Dodge. On April 28, Forrest reported to Johnston that there were ten thousand men facing him and Roddey, and there was "a heavy column threatening his left."[107] He now had to make the most important decision of the campaign. Either late on the twenty-eighth or early on the twenty-ninth at Courtland, he decided to let Dodge go and pursue the force the scouts had seen. He must have been angry, even enraged, that he had been drawn into a profitless and time-consuming skirmish at Town Creek. Although he still did not know the Yankees' intentions, he quickly gave orders, preparing for hard riding to make up for lost time. But it was still too early to bring his force together. He ordered Dibrell to stay at Florence. He also sent most of Morton's battery to Florence, keeping only two rifled guns under Lieutenant Willis Gould. The 5th and 53rd Alabama, from Roddey's command, were ordered to watch Dodge. Roddey, with Julian's Battalion and the 11th Tennessee, was to get on Streight's trail and pursue him from the west. Forrest, with the 4th and 9th Tennessee, Morton's lightest guns double-teamed, and Captain George Ferrell's six-gun Georgia Artillery from Roddey's command, would head for Moulton, a little less than twenty miles to the south. Three days' rations were prepared. Marching orders were for 1:00 a.m. on the twenty-ninth. Streight had left Moulton an hour earlier.[108]

Streight was heading into country far different than the Tennessee Valley to which Dodge was laying waste. Though not mountainous, the Alabama hill country is high and rugged. Rucker Agee, who went over the campaign trail in the early 1950s, described the region well: "In 1863 the region was sparsely settled. There were few roadways, the roads largely followed the ridges and crossed the streams only at a limited number of fords…[This was] before there was a Cullman County or an L&N Railroad or a city of Birmingham [ninety miles southeast of Moulton], before there was a paved highway or steel bridge or even a graded road on Sand Mountain."[109] There were no large plantations, though slaves did attach themselves to the Federal column from time to time. Even today, the country has an air of isolation about it, especially on the long climb of twenty-five miles from Moulton to Sand Mountain. The region then was heavily forested. Agee noted in 1958 that "the great forests were gone," replaced by second growth "spotted by pastures and fields…Old timers state that in the early days, the virgin forest of great pines and oaks, with some poplar, hickory, gum, chestnut, and sycamore formed a roof which shut out the sunlight and retarded the growth of underbrush to such an extent that a deer could be seen for half a mile."[110]

Many of the men from the region were away with the 20th Alabama under Pemberton at Vicksburg, but for Captain D.D. Smith's two companies of Alabama Union cavalry, this region was home. Smith's men were Streight's scouts, guides, vanguard, and rearguard. They saw friends and family along the road and throughout the country.[111]

As day dawned on the twenty-ninth, the sun bid fair for dry weather, "which gave us strong hope of better things," Streight wrote.[112] The brigade made good progress on an uneventful day, making camp at the foot of Sand Mountain, on the main road just below Day's Gap. The road through the Gap was an old Indian trail, one of several more or less parallel roads up the mountain.

Forrest had ridden into Moulton about twelve hours after Streight left. He learned that the enemy had taken the road to Sand Mountain. He decided to ride on all night, but he was still unsure of the enemy's intention. Therefore, he ordered Roddey, who had rejoined the command, to stay on Streight's trail with the 4th Alabama, Julian's Battalion, the 11th Tennessee, and Captain Ferrell's battery. Forrest, Forrest's escort, Captain William Forrest's scouts, and Lieutenant E. Willis Gould's section of Morton's battery moved toward Danville, about five miles from Day's Gap. Forrest sent the 4th and 9th Tennessee farther north, either to prevent Streight from breaking back in that direction or to cut him off east of Day's Gap on the main road.[113]

By the time Streight made camp that night, he had ridden 75 miles since leaving Tuscumbia on April 26. Forrest, in pursuit, had covered 140 miles since leaving Spring Hill, Tennessee, very early on the twenty-fourth.[114] Streight probably did not know that he was being pursued. But before light, Forrest's scouts had located the Union camp. One scout wrote that they didn't need to see it—they could hear it. W.G. Wilkins explained: "Just before daylight [April 30], there broke out the most awful noise…in one mighty effort, nearly 2,000 mules, braying in far-reaching and penetrating chorus, set the echoes of vibration among the Alabama mountains."[115]

Forrest planned quickly: Biffle (9th Tennessee) and McLemore (4th Tennessee) might be able to get onto the road east of the Gap, perhaps trapping Streight between their troops and his. He sent his brother's scouts forward and made ready to advance behind them.

Streight broke camp early, before first light. While the infantry prepared to ride out, Captain Smith, commanding the rear guard, posted pickets as the rest of his men started fires and began to brew coffee. The day dawned fair again. Lieutenant A.C. Roach, Streight's aide-de-camp, wrote, "The sun shone out bright and beautiful as a spring day's sun ever beamed, and from the smoldering camp fires of the previous night mild blue smoke mingled with the gray mist on the mountain tops above."[116]

William Forrest's scouts stealthily approached the camps, capturing the unsuspecting pickets and moving to within four hundred yards of the breakfast fires. Lieutenant Gould brought up his guns close behind and opened fire. "I heard the boom of the artillery," wrote Streight, who was then two miles up the road. The rear guard scattered, racing to reach the rear of the column. Streight made a quick and good decision. He was aware of the smaller roads running parallel to his and was afraid he might be flanked and trapped. He decided not to make a stand where he was, at or near the crest of Sand Mountain, but to push on and find better ground with a better line of retreat. According to Ed Bearss, "Colonel Streight had shown a keen appreciation of terrain in selecting this strong position. Nobody will quarrel with the colonel's skillful dispositions."[117] He soon found ground to his liking, with a ravine protecting his left flank and a marshy run on his right. The 73rd Indiana went into line of battle on the left, with the 51st Indiana, the 3rd Ohio, and the 80th Illinois extending the line to the marshy run. The two howitzers unlimbered on either side of the road.

Streight most likely expected and hoped for a headlong cavalry charge. But Forrest's men were used to fighting dismounted. "We had lost our shotguns in Kentucky," wrote Whitsitt, "and henceforth fought chiefly as infantry."[118] Streight gave orders not to fire until the last of Smith's troopers rode through the infantry line. When Forrest came up, he immediately dismounted the 11th Tennessee and put his escort on its left. But Roddey's men, riding hard, veered toward Streight's left and charged. The Hoosiers held their fire until they could fire point blank. The Confederates had been drawn "into a deadly trap…We were surprised and knocked out of formation."[119] Forty riders went down killed or wounded. William Forrest was severely wounded, shot in the thigh. In a gallant attempt to cover their wild retreat, Lieutenant Gould advanced his guns too far forward—within three hundred yards of the Yankee line. Before they could get the range—they fired too high at first—Streight ordered the 3rd Ohio and the 80th Illinois to charge. They drove back the 11th Tennessee and charged Gould's guns. Because most of the horses had been killed, Gould abandoned his guns. Forrest was infuriated, livid with rage. Thomas Duncan, who had been with Forrest from the beginning of the War, wrote, "It was the only time in my entire service of four years with Forrest that I ever saw him perturbed. He was as furious and as wild as a lion."[120] The two guns Streight had taken were part of Forrest's haul at Murfreesboro the previous June.[121] Forrest blamed Gould for their loss, with dire consequences for both men.

Streight did not press his advantage but fell back to his original position, dragging Gould's guns back to his mountain howitzers. What followed was "an animated skirmish between the sharpshooters of both forces until 3:00 p.m."[122] Biffle and McLemore had been unable to get on the main road east of Streight and had returned to the main force. Forrest then prepared a general assault, dismounted, but by about 11:00 a.m., Streight had pulled out.

The casualties at Day's Gap are difficult to determine. Between sixty and seventy killed and wounded for Forrest seems to be a reasonable figure.[123] The Union surgeon William Spencer listed Streight's casualties as eleven killed, thirty-nine wounded (ten later died), and twenty-four captured. Spencer would bury the Union dead "in a small graveyard in what is now Battleground, Alabama [Day's Gap]." Robert Willett thinks that it may be in the Day's Old War Cemetery "just northwest of Battleground, just over the line into Morgan County." Lieutenant J.W. Pavey, Streight's artillerist, was badly wounded. Colonel James W. Sheets, of the 51st Indiana, was mortally wounded.

The fight at Day's Gap brings out the deadly nature of Streight's mission and Forrest's pursuit. "War means fighting," Forrest once said, and "fighting means killing."

Forrest lost about thirty minutes at Day's Gap after Streight pulled out. It took that long to get his men remounted. He also gave new orders: Roddey was to take his men, the wounded, and the prisoners to Decatur. Captain George Ferrell's battery would stay with Forrest. He sent Edmondson's 11th Tennessee toward Summerville, on Streight's left. For the rest of the chase, that force remained on Streight's left, between the Federals and the Tennessee River. Recurrent reports about this force, whose size and identity he did not know, worried Streight. He had no intention of recrossing the Tennessee River, but the Confederates could, he feared, get between him and Blountsville, Gadsden, or even Rome.[124]

Forrest kept up the pressure with the rest—escorts, scouts, and most of the 4th and 9th Tennessee—about one thousand men. Whitsitt remembered him saying, "Shoot at anything blue, and keep up the scare."[125]

"Streight made a stand at every creek or stream," wrote Lieutenant R.W. Jones, one of Captain Ferrell's gunners.[126] The most hotly contested crossing was at Crooked Creek, about seven miles from Day's Gap, "a narrow, rocky, vividly green mountain stream" flowing between steep banks high on each side down to the ford.[127] The site of the ford is the most imposing location along the entire raid route. If you walk down to the ford from today's Crooked Creek Civil War Museum, you'll pass gun pits dug into the steep slopes.

Crooked Creek and Hog Mountain - April 30, 1862

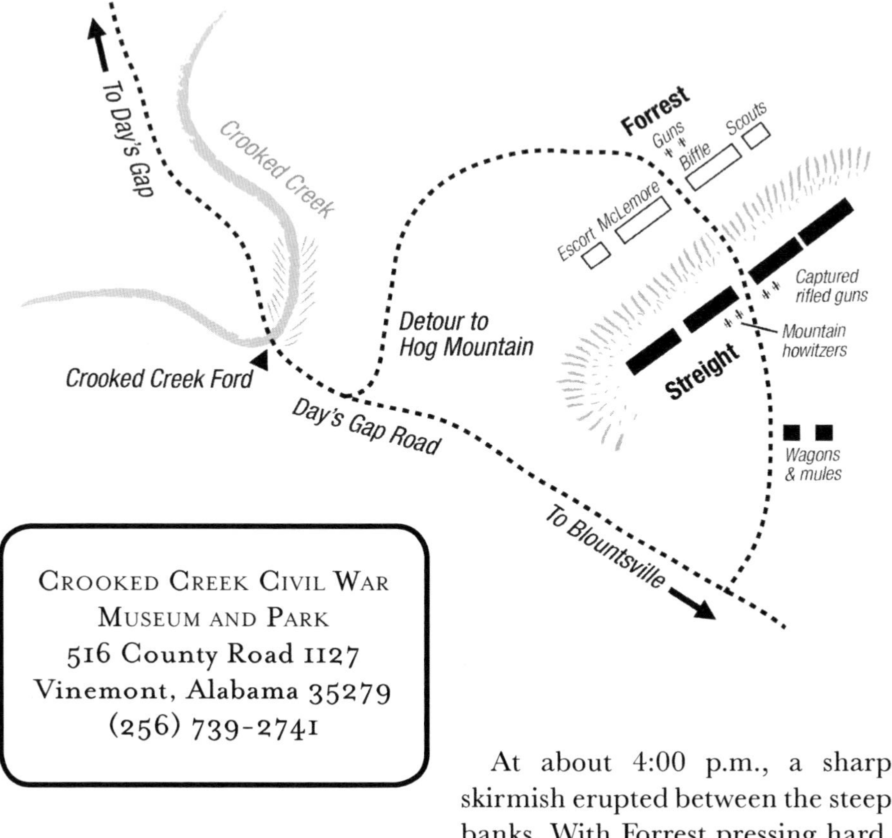

CROOKED CREEK CIVIL WAR MUSEUM AND PARK
516 County Road 1127
Vinemont, Alabama 35279
(256) 739-2741

At about 4:00 p.m., a sharp skirmish erupted between the steep banks. With Forrest pressing hard, Streight crossed his artillery first. As the column made its way across, the two mountain howitzers and Gould's captured guns took up positions to lay down a covering fire. The infantry came across as quickly as it could. The horses and mules came down to the ford readily enough—they were thirsty and smelled or heard the water. Getting them in the creek was easy, but the mules, especially, balked at going on. They wanted to drink deeply. With time slipping away, Streight put the 73rd Indiana and the 3rd Ohio in close support of the guns. The artillery kept the Confederates back long enough to complete the crossing. When the column cleared the stream, the 73rd Indiana and some of Smith's command formed a rear guard. They slowed the Confederates enough for Streight to find good ground at Hog Mountain, about two miles from Crooked Creek, for another stand.

"Scattered over the [Sand Mountain] plateau are little ridges and elevated places called by the natives 'Sugar Loaf' mountains. Such is Hog Mountain,"[128] wrote Rucker Agee.

Streight's position on Hog Mountain overlooked the road. About an hour before dark, Streight put his men in line of battle, two regiments on either side of the road, at the crest, with the four guns at the center. An informative Civil War Trust marker stands at the site today.

Coming on from Crooked Creek, Forrest reined in as soon as the ground began to rise sharply. The men who had charged headlong at Day's Gap were no longer with him. It was dark, or nearly so, by the time he aligned his men for an assault. He put McLemore and his escort on his right, Biffle and the scouts on his left. In the fierce struggle, three of Forrest's horses were killed beneath him. In hand-to-hand fighting, lit up by the flashes of artillery and rifle fire, Streight's line held. "This was the first night battle I had witnessed," wrote Whitsitt. "The pine trees were very tall, the darkness of their shade very intense…the mountain was steep as we charged again and again under Forrest's own lead. It was a great spectacle."[129] The bitter intensity of the fighting only reinforced Streight's notion that he was heavily outnumbered. His ever-present fear of being cut off set in again, and at about 10:00 p.m., he withdrew on the road to Blountsville, about thirty miles away.

When Forrest's men reached the crest, they found the dismal aftermath of an abandoned position: Gould's two guns, left behind but spiked (Streight had no more ammunition for them); the dead; and the men too badly wounded to be moved (Union casualties seem to have been about thirty-five men killed and wounded). It was here that the Confederates encountered Union surgeon William Spencer, left behind to bury the dead and tend to the wounded. Spencer's account, in the collection of the Indiana Historical Society, is mostly a description of his captivity in Libby Prison, in Richmond. His description of what happened at Hog Mountain seems more fiction than fact. He claimed that Forrest lost three hundred men killed at Hog Mountain and that Forrest's officers kept this knowledge from the six hundred or so survivors. He also said that when he spoke to Forrest, Forrest was riding in a carriage. He described Forrest's soldiers as a "a mongrel set of armed men and illiterate." Forrest was "a pleasant good-looking man," brimming with compliments for Streight's men and for Spencer staying behind with the wounded.

"I felt as though such urbanity and evidence of good breeding and generosity to our unfortunate wounded was worthy a better cause than that of destroying the best government on Earth." Spencer remembered Forrest saying that "the

South had no quarrel with Indiana or any of the other western states, but only with the 'pestiferous presence of the blue-bellied Abolition Yankees.'"

Spencer summed up by saying, "I found the men and officers had great respect for General Forrest, which was intermingled with a little wholesome fear...altogether he makes a better fight with his ragamuffins than one would suppose."[130]

The conversation could not have lasted more than a brief moment or two. Spencer had severely wounded patients to treat and the dead to bury.

Spencer remained free to tend to his men until May 19, when he was sent north to Libby Prison, in Richmond, Virginia. His patients had a rough road to recovery, if they recovered at all. But "one saving grace for the injured was the presence of friendly civilians." It is likely that not every civilian who came forward to help the doctor and his nurses was a Unionist, but most were. "This was one of their first opportunities to show their sympathy for not just the Union cause, but for the soldiers who offered up their lives and limbs for the same cause."[131] It was the largest and most telling expression of Alabama Unionism during the raid, but it came after the Federal column had departed, heading east.

Forrest took up the chase again. "There was constant peril of ambuscade," Whitsitt wrote, "but we waited for the moon to rise before pressing close upon the enemy."[132] Warily, Forrest "strung out" his men, with a few in the lead, the most dangerous position. Cavalrymen helped the gunners pull the cannon forward, because horses would have been too loud for safety.[133]

Streight's rear guard was now Colonel Hathaway's 73rd Indiana. Streight rode with the colonel. They laid two ambushes during the night. The first is known as Hathaway's Ambush, and the second may be the skirmish at Ryan's Creek, shown on the Civil War Trust's map.[134] Accounts differ as to how successful they were. In one, Granville Pillow, one of Biffle's men, got close enough to the Yankee rear guard to overhear Union officers' orders. He alerted Forrest in time. Forrest then ordered the guns brought forward. In both ambushes, the artillery, firing canister, soon cleared Hathaway's men out of the roadside thickets and timber. Forrest kept pushing until about three o'clock in the morning. His men, and especially his horses, were worn out. From this point on, especially after daybreak, Streight had one advantage: he could commandeer fresh horses, either from roadside fields or from carriages and wagons encountered on the road to Blountsville.

Streight did not rest during the night but kept going until he reached Blountsville at about 10:00 a.m. That day, May 1, 1863, was going to be "the liveliest day in the history of Blountsville."[135]

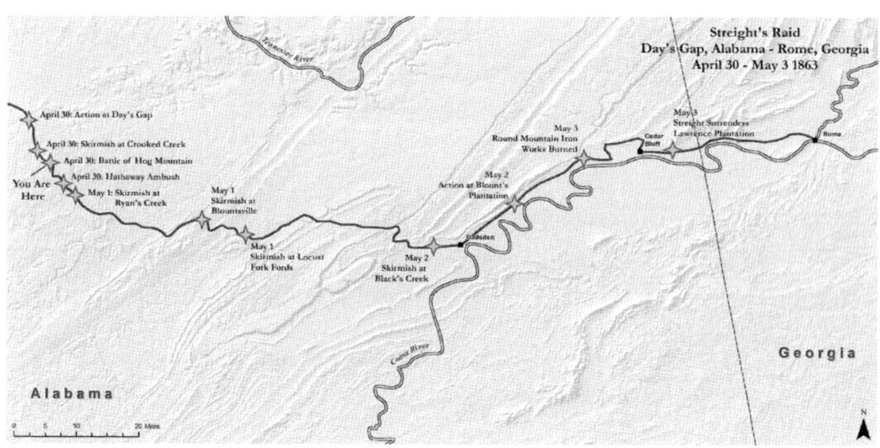

From the Civil War Trust's marker at Hog Mountain. *Civil War Trust.*

The raiders reached Blountsville in good order with the column closed up. Men and animals needed rest, and Streight wanted to lighten the load. He ordered his men to empty five of the six wagons, burn them, and pack the ammunition and hardtack onto mules. Apparently, Colonel Hathaway was the only one who knew how to secure the packs with either a single or double diamond hitch knot.[136]

The men found—or may have been led to—corn and other forage. They burned all other supplies to keep them from Forrest. Streight also decided to forbid the refugee slaves with the column from going on any farther. They were slowing him down, and he had to move fast. With five fewer wagons, some rest, and some forage, he might be able to gain on the pursuit.

It was a vain hope. He had no sooner given the orders to mount and ride out than Forrest was on him again. "The column had not gotten fairly under motion before our pickets were driven in and a sharp skirmish ensued between Forrest's advance and our rear guard, under Captain Smith, in the town of Blountsville itself."[137] When Forrest drew rein in Blountsville, the wagons were still burning, near the Blountsville Cemetery.[138]

As he rode east, Streight may have reflected on his plight. He had fought two pitched engagements and been in a running fight since leaving Day's Gap thirty miles behind. He had no choice but to stop at Blountsville, even if only for an hour or so. Forrest was slashing Streight's rear guard again with what Streight believed to be a force much larger than his own. He had one hundred miles to go before reaching Rome and another eighteen before reaching the W&A Railroad. He did not know how kind Alabama Unionists had been to Dr. Spencer and his patients; all he knew was that they had been very little help to him. In fairness, however, a column passing through, riding mules, hotly pursued, heading for Georgia, would not have inspired much confidence in civilians anyway. Back on April 28, trooper Stanton Brumfield had described the brigade as "a band of guerillas."[139] It was not going to get any better as Streight neared Gadsden and the fertile Coosa River Valley. He was far from any Union force, and even his own Alabamians were moving farther away from their homes, neighbors, and Unionist friends.

It is probably just as well that Streight did not know how much help Confederate loyalists were giving Forrest. The story of Celia and Winnie May Murphree, famous in North Alabama, is a good example. As Streight headed for Royal Ford, about seven miles from Blountsville, to cross the east branch of the Black Warrior River (on the Civil War Trust map labeled Locust Fork Ford), two of his soldiers left the column, looking for horses. They came to the cabin of Arminda Reed Murphree. Her husband was a Confederate soldier and away in the army. She had just given birth to a baby. Her sisters, Celia, twenty-one, and Winnie, eighteen, were with her. The soldiers came up to the cabin, killed two mule colts, and began ransacking the barn. They seized two mares. Then, barging into the house, they demanded "spirits." They found a jug—of something—intended as a painkiller for Arminda. They mockingly demanded mint juleps. The sisters served up two sinister creations, blends of the painkiller and some patent medicine for toothaches. When the soldiers came to, they found themselves looking down the barrels of their own rifles in the hands of the sisters, now joined by a brother.[140]

While the foragers were sleeping it off at the Murphree cabin, Streight had gotten across Royal Ford. A heavy skirmish line held the Confederates back long enough for the column to get across. Two mules, weighed down with hardtack, slipped and drowned. By early afternoon, Streight was on his way to Walnut Grove, which he reached at mid-afternoon. He kept on from there.

Forrest crossed Royal Ford right behind Streight and followed him toward Walnut Grove. He reached there by late afternoon on May 1. Unlike Streight, however, Forrest decided to rest most of his men for most of the night. He sent 150 men ahead to stay close to Streight but gave most of the men and horses their first real rest in three days. It was here that the Murphrees brought in their 2 prisoners. Forrest gave them a mare to compensate for the loss of the two mules.

Streight paused briefly near today's Atalla, Alabama, and then moved on to the next obstacle, Wills Creek, seven miles from Gadsden. At this point he left behind men too sick or hurt to go on any farther, together with more slaves who had joined the column east of Blountsville. There was more to Streight's decision to abandon the slaves than just quickening the pace. Even if he reached Rome and then the W&A, being captured was a strong possibility. Having slaves with the column could be as lethally dangerous to Streight's men as being captured in civilian clothing had been to Andrews' men.

The crossing was difficult. Even the sure-footed mules had trouble. Their packs were loose, and a lot of the ammunition packs slipped and toppled into the creek. Forrest captured about twenty-five prisoners.[111] He also pared down his command. He then sent the twenty-five prisoners back to Decatur and went ahead with perhaps six hundred men and two guns.[112]

"Until Streight reached Gadsden, it was always possible that he might turn northwest toward the rear of the Confederate forces in the Tennessee Valley. However, proceeding northeast from Gadsden, Streight was hemmed in on the right by the Coosa and on the left by Lookout Mountain. There was no route except along the old Cherokee Indian trail toward the railroads of northwest Georgia.[113]

At about 8:00 a.m., Forrest dashed off a dispatch for a courier to deliver to whomever he thought best in Rome. It is probably the only example of a Forrest dispatch in his own unedited words:

> *To the authoritys of Rome Georgia theirs is a Federal Force of fifteen Hundred cavalry Marching on your place I am pressing them Prepare your selves to Repuls them—they have 2 Mountain Howitsers I will be clost on them I have kild 300 of their men they air runing for their lives*
>
> *N.B. Forrest*
> *Brig Genl*
> *Cavalry North Ala*[114]

Chapter 6

Emma Sansom and the Low Water Ford

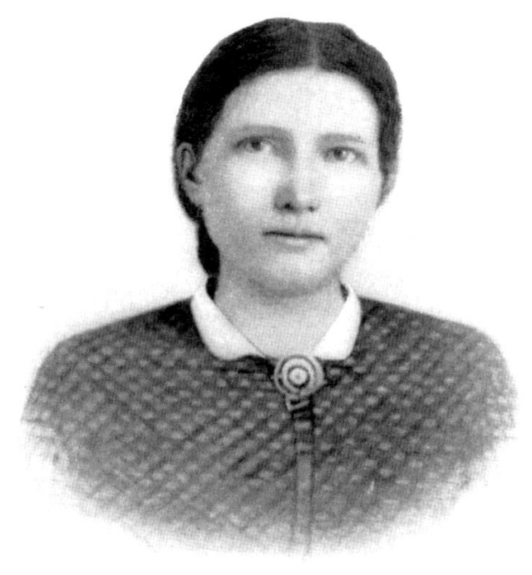

Emma Sansom, as she was frequently pictured in the *Confederate Veterans* magazine. *Alabama Department of Archives and History, Montgomery, Alabama.*

It was about 8:00 a.m. on May 2 when Streight neared Black Creek on the Old Tuscaloosa Road, about two miles west of Gadsden. In 1899, John Allan Wyeth described Black Creek well in his biography of Forrest: "Black Creek is a crooked, deep, and sluggish stream with precipitous clay banks and mud bottom. It has its source on the plateau of Lookout Mountain, the southern limit of which range is less than one mile to the north. Only a little further away, in a series of precipitous falls and whirling cascades, pure and crystal white a mountain stream leaping from rock to rock it falls from its high estate to mingle with the stained and muddy waters of the lowlands."[145] In late April 1863, it had rained a lot, and the creek was high.[146] A bridge carried the Old Tuscaloosa Road over the creek. There was also a ford, although neither Streight nor Forrest knew about it.[147]

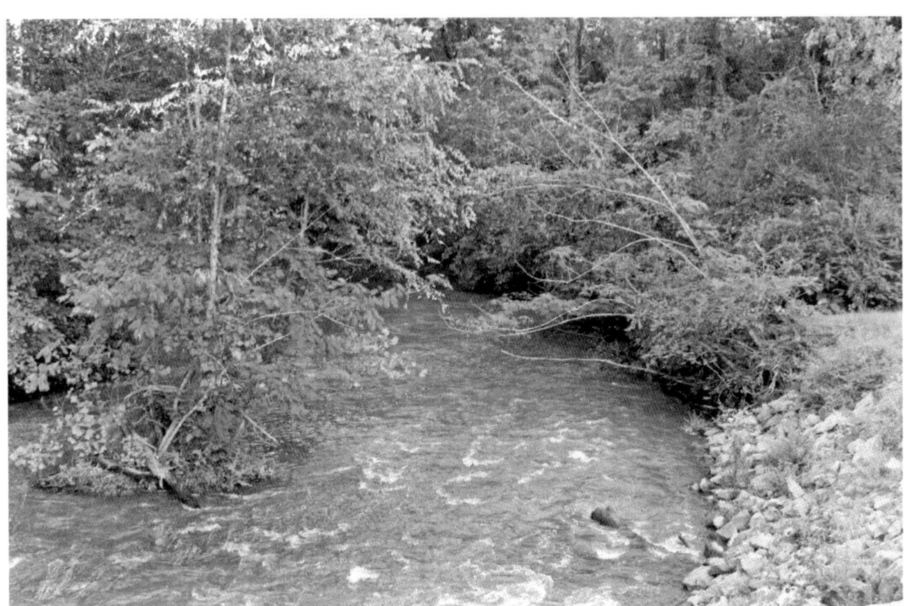

A view of Black Creek, 2015. *Bob Price, photographer.*

Although Forrest was close, Streight had enough time to cross the bridge and then burn it behind him. Finally—he should be able to put some time and distance between his worn-down men and the relentless Confederates.

When Forrest rode up to the bridge, it was already impassable. Had Streight escaped him? There seemed no way to avoid a crippling, lengthy delay. Was there any way to cross Black Creek?

Since July 4, 1907, a statue of a young girl has stood at what is now the west end of Broad Street in Gadsden at the foot of the modern bridge over the Coosa River. The young girl is Emma Sansom (1847–1900).[118] In May 1863, she was fifteen, living with her mother, Lamila, and her sister, Mary Jane (Jennie), in a farm cabin on the west bank of Black Creek, about nine hundred yards from the bridge over Black Creek. Her arm is outstretched—she is showing the way across Black Creek.

Emma's father had died in 1859. The family may have owned a slave, Fannie, who had been with them for many years. Emma had six brothers, at least five of whom were Confederate soldiers. One brother, Rufus, had been wounded in battle and may have been in the Gadsden area recuperating, but if he was, he was not at home that morning. Emma's friend Mary Blair, eleven years old, who lived close by, was with Emma.

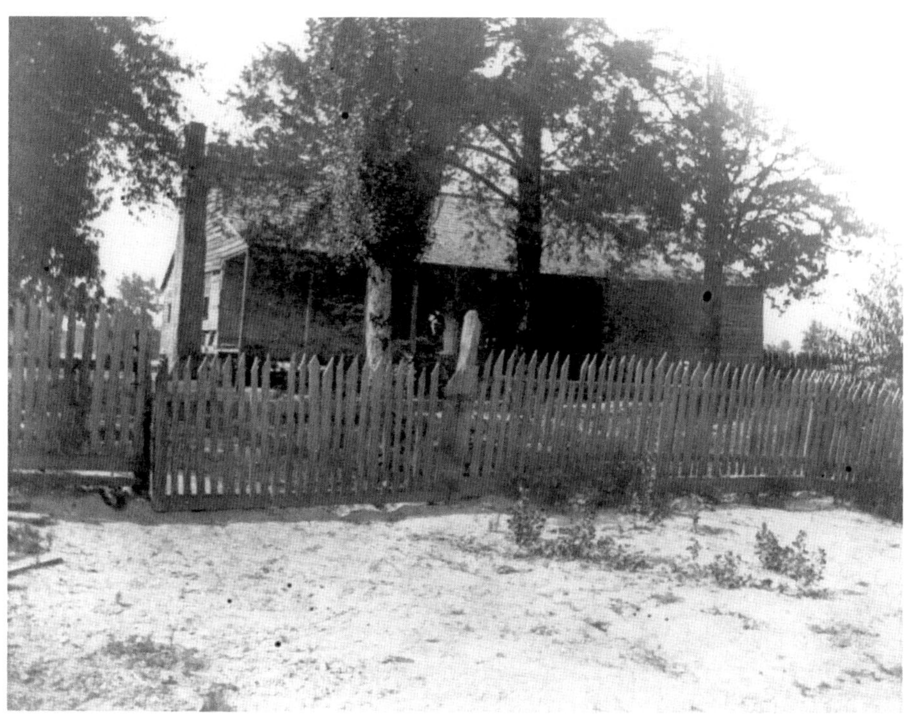

The Sansom house as it appeared until the 1930s. The house was on a rise five hundred yards due west of Black Creek and about nine hundred yards from the bridge Streight burned. The site today is the southeast corner of the gym of the Emma Sansom Middle School. *Etowah County Historical Society; Larry Johnson, personal collection.*

Thirty-three years later, in 1896, Emma wrote a description of what happened on May 2 for Dr. John A. Wyeth, whose biography of Forrest was published in 1899. She wrote:

> *We were at home on the morning of May 2, 1863, when about eight or nine o'clock a company of men wearing blue uniforms and riding mules and horses galloped past the house and went on towards the bridge. Pretty soon a great crowd of them came along, and some of them stopped at the gate and asked us to bring them some water. Sister and I each took a bucket of water, and gave it them at the gate. One of them asked me where my father was. I told him he was dead. He asked me if I had any brothers. I told him I had "six." He asked where they were, and I told him they were in the Confederate Army...*
>
> *By this time some of them began to dismount, and we went into the house. They came in and began to search for fire-arms and men's*

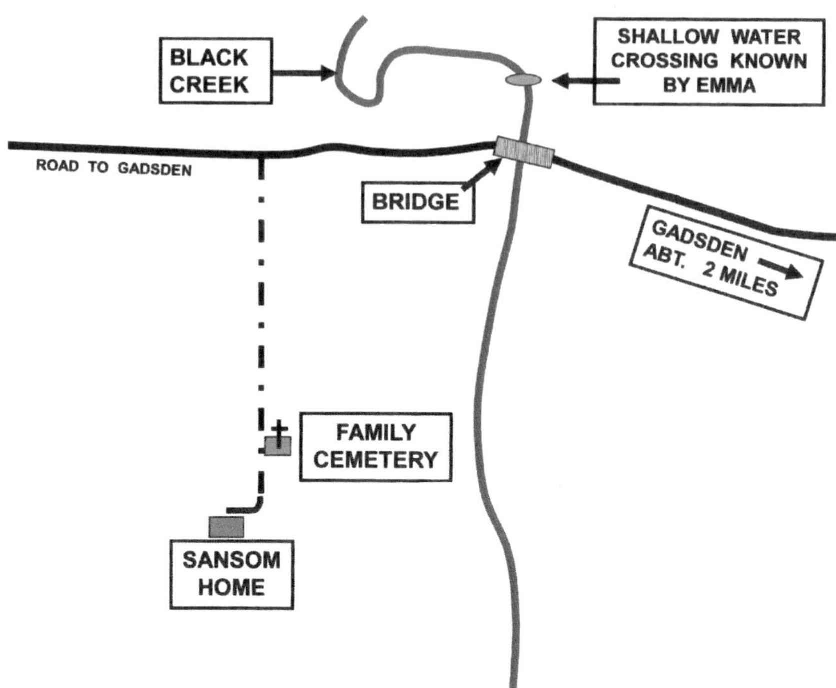

The low water ford is about two hundred yards upstream from the bridge Streight burned, which is also the site of the present bridge. Forrest and Emma rode to the ford, skirting the high ground on the west bank, and then went down a ravine, part of the way on foot, to the place where Emma Sansom showed Forrest the low water ford. *Larry Johnson.*

saddles. They did not find anything but a side-saddle, and one of them cut the skirts off that. Just then someone from the road said in a loud tone: "You men bring a chunk of fire with you and get out of that house." The men got the fire in the kitchen and started out, and an officer put a guard around the house, saying: "This guard is for your protection." They all soon hurried down to the bridge, and in a few minutes we saw the smoke rising and knew they were burning the bridge. As our fence extended up to the railing of the bridge, mother said: "Come with me and we will pull our rails away so they will not be destroyed." As we got to the top of the hill we saw the rails were already piled on the bridge and were on fire, and the Yankees were in line on the other side guarding it.

We turned back towards the house, and had not gone but a few steps before we saw a Yankee coming at full speed, and behind were some

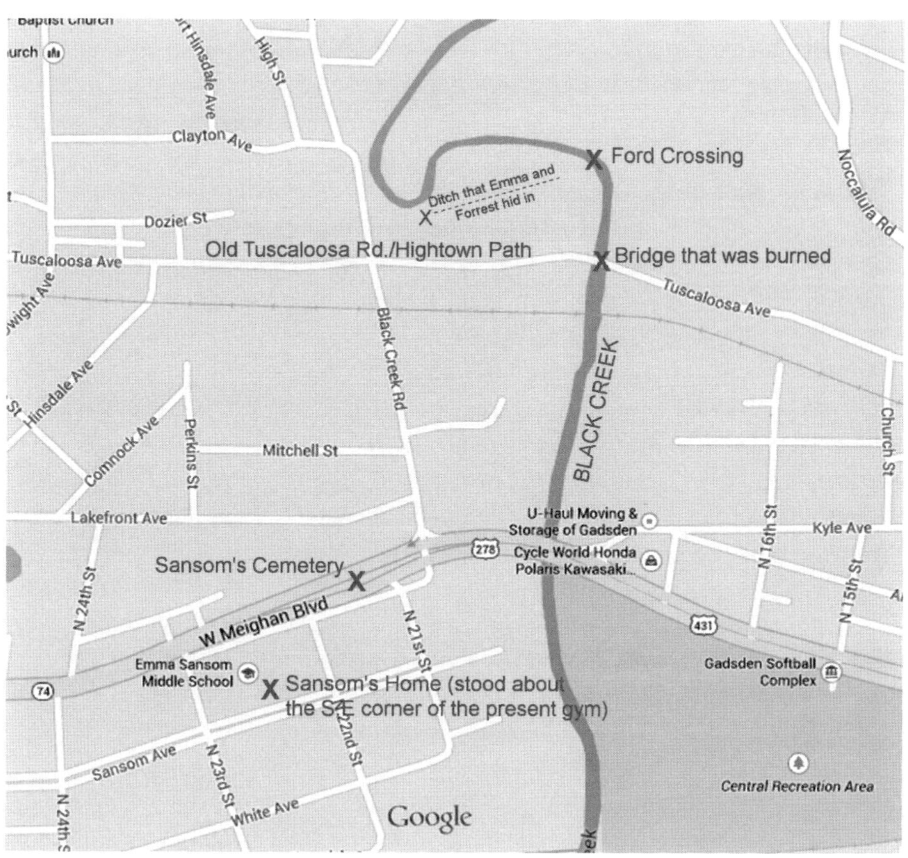

Modern-day overlay onto the May 1863 map. *Danny Crownover, Etowah County Historical Society.*

more men on horses. I heard them shout, "Halt and surrender!" The man stopped, threw up his hand, and handed over his gun. The officer to whom the soldier surrendered said: "Ladies, do not be alarmed, I am General Forrest; I and my men will protect you from harm." He inquired: "Where are the Yankees?" Mother said: "They have set the bridge on fire and are standing in line on the other side, and if you go down that hill they will kill the last one of you." By this time our men had come up, and some went out in the field, and both sides commenced shooting. We ran to the house, and I got there ahead of all.

General Forrest dashed up to the gate and said to me: "Can you tell me where I can get across that creek?" I told him there was an unsafe bridge two miles farther down the stream, but that I knew of a trail about two hundred yards above the bridge on our farm, where our cows

> *used to cross in low water, and I believed he could get his men over there, and that if he would have my saddle put on a horse I would show him the way. He said: "There's no time to saddle a horse; get up here behind me." As he said this he rode close to the bank on the side of the road, and I jumped up behind him. Just as we started off, mother came up about out of breath and gasped out: "Emma, what do you mean?" General Forrest said: "She is going to show me a ford where I can get my men over in time to catch those Yankees before they get to Rome. Don't be uneasy; I will bring her back safe."*

Forrest did not ride directly down to the bridge. There were still Federals on the high ground on the opposite bank. Forrest and Emma would have been within their firing range. Instead, as directed by Emma, Forrest skirted high ground on the near bank to approach the ford, two hundred yards north of the bridge, out of sight of the Federals.

> *We rode out into a field through which ran a branch or small ravine and along which there was a thick undergrowth that protected us for a while from being seen by the Yankees at the bridge or on the other side of the creek. This branch emptied into the creek just above the ford. I said: "General Forrest, I think we had better get off the horse, as we are now where we may be seen." We both got down and crept through the bushes, and when we were right at the ford I happened to be in front. He stepped quickly between me and the Yankees, saying: "I'm glad to have you for a pilot, but I'm not going to make breastworks of you." The cannon and the other guns were firing fast by this time, as I pointed out to him where to go into the water and out on the other bank, and then we went back towards the house.*
>
> *He asked me my name, and asked me to give him a lock of my hair. The cannon-balls were screaming over us so loud that we were told to leave and hide in some place out of danger, which we did. Soon all the firing stopped, and I started back home. On the way I met General Forrest again, and he told me that he had written a note for me and left it on the bureau. He asked me again for a lock of my hair, and as we went into the house he said: "One of my bravest men has been killed, and he is laid out in the house. His name is Robert Turner. I want you to see that he is buried in some graveyard near here." He then told me good-bye and got on his horse, and he and his men rode away and left us all alone. My sister and I sat up all night watching over the dead*

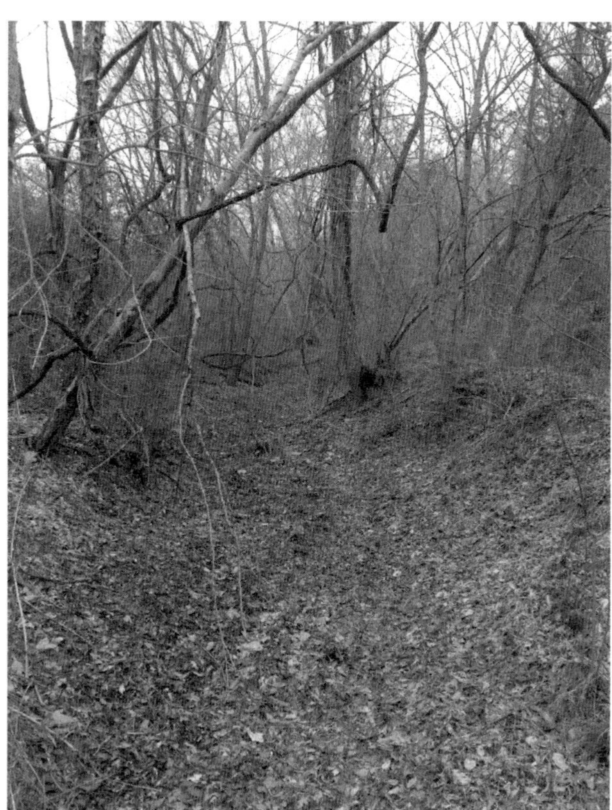

Right: Forrest shielded Emma as they came down this ravine to the ford. *Melissa W. Beck, photographer.*

Below: A view of the ford taken in the late nineteenth century. *Larry Johnson, personal collection.*

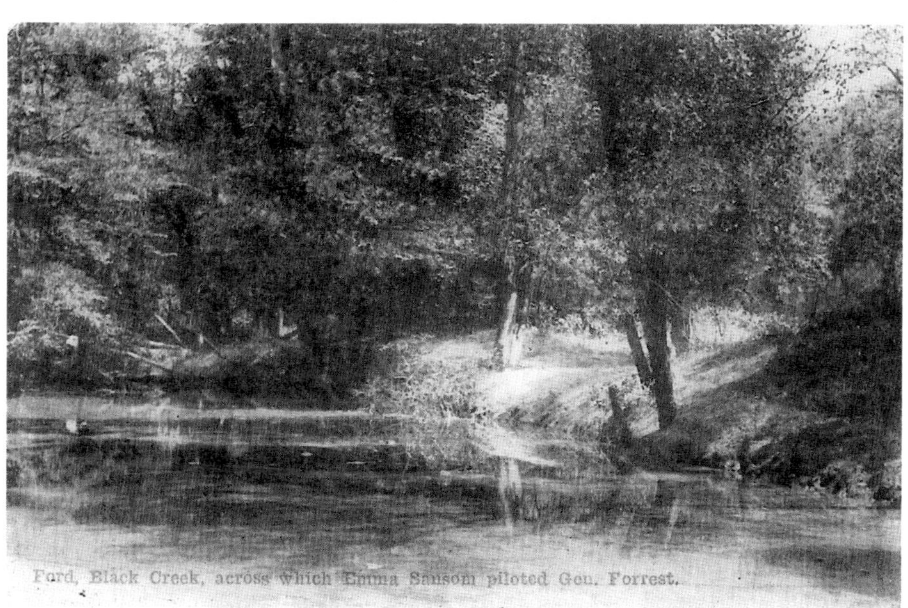

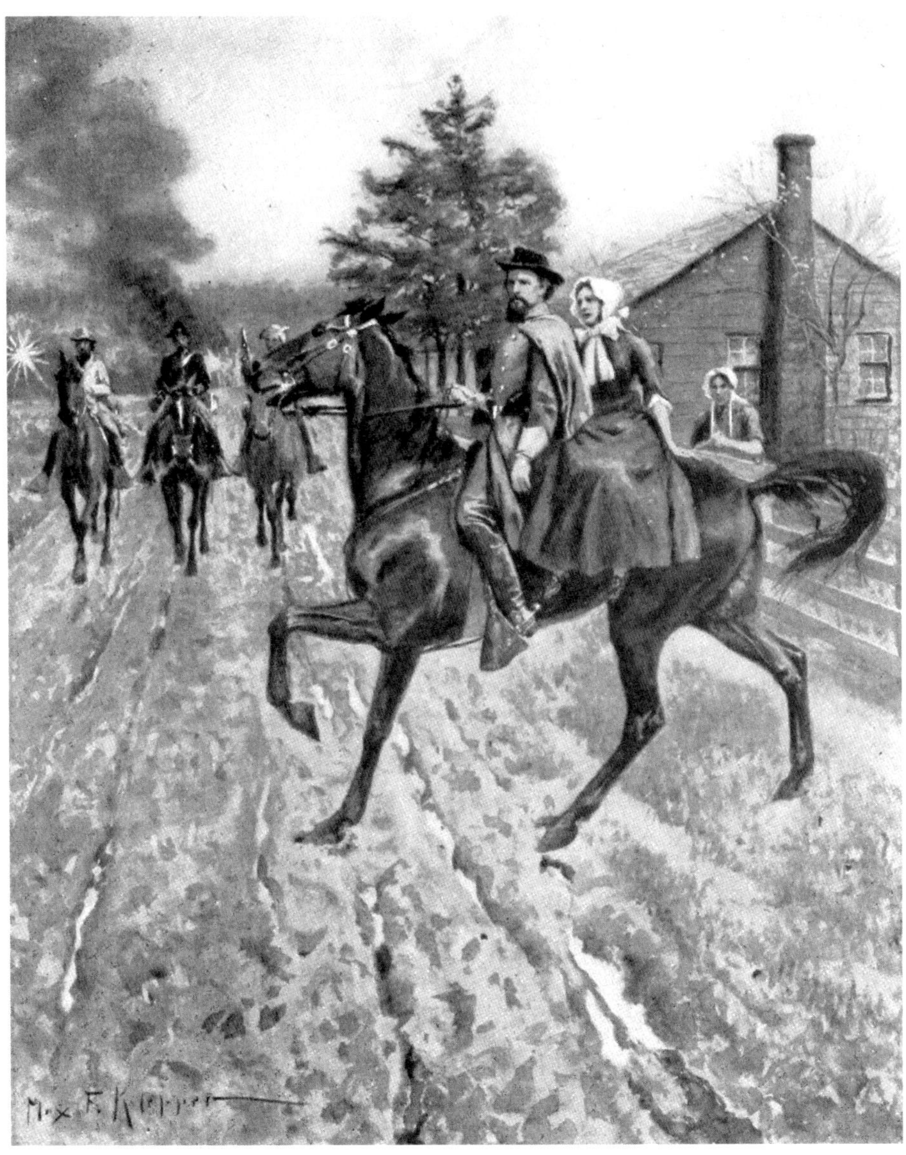

Emma could truthfully say that she "rode with Forrest." She never sought publicity or profit for riding with the general and showing him the way over Black Creek. It was not until her own account appeared in Dr. Wyeth's biography of Forrest (1899) that she took her rightful place in history.

> *soldier, who had lost his life fighting for our rights, in which we were overpowered but never conquered. General Forrest and his men endeared themselves to us forever.*[119]

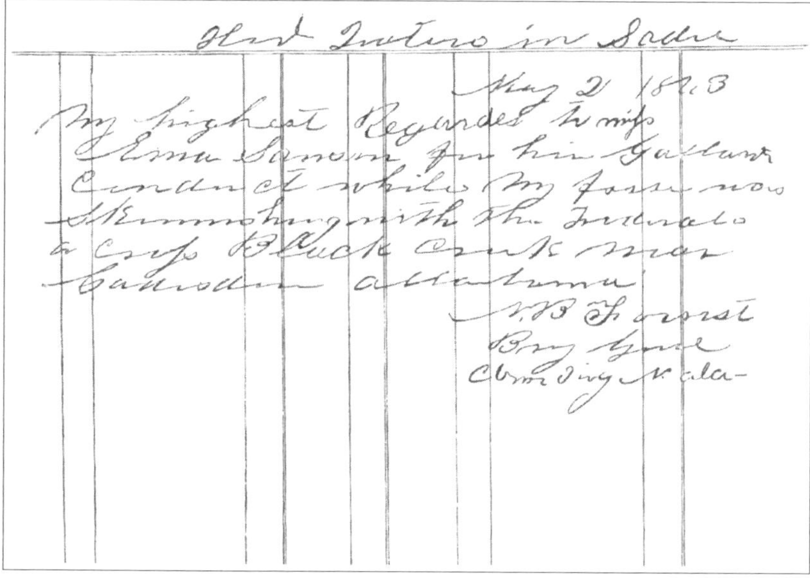

The note Forrest left Emma on her mother's bureau. Emma probably gave the note to Dr. Wyeth; its whereabouts today are unknown. *Larry Johnson, personal collection.*

Hed Quarters in Sadle
May 2, 1863

My highest Regardes to Miss Emma Sanson for her Gallant Conduct while my forse was Skirmishing with the Federals across Black Creek near Gadsden Allabama.

N. B Forrest
Brig. Genrl
Comding N. Ala[150]

Naturally, a number of stories swirl around this historical event. In one, it was a sergeant in the 20th Alabama, not Forrest, who escorted Emma home from the ford. Also, Emma's brother Rufus is involved in other tellings of the story. Both are unlikely. However, a member of Forrest's escort, R.C. Garrett, of Unionville, Tennessee, recalled seeing Emma sitting behind Forrest as they rode down to the ford.[151]

In 1939, Emma's friend Mary Blair, then Mrs. Mary Blair McKinnon, wrote to Mary Harrison Lister, a Gadsden historian, responding to an article Lister had published in the *Gadsden Times*. Mary was eleven in 1863. Her eyewitness account essentially agrees with Emma's. She did say that she had

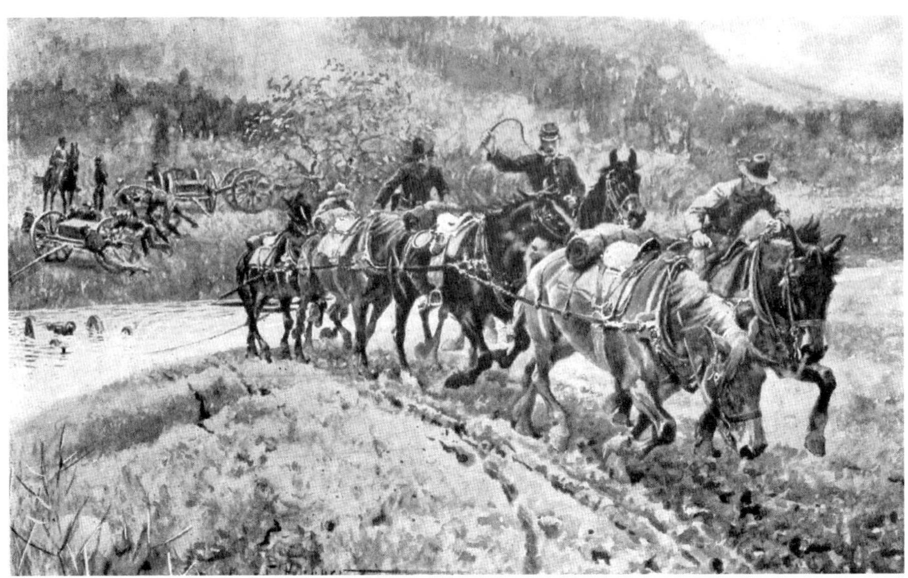

Eight horses, struggling mightily to pull one of Forrest's guns over Black Creek. Two caissons and another gun remain on the west bank. Taken from *Wyeth's Life of Lieutenant General Forrest* (1899).

not seen Federal soldiers cutting open the family's feather beds despite the heated and anguished protests of Lizzie or Fannie. Neither did Emma. Mary had heard the story many times over the years. She said she saw Emma on Forrest's horse, and she described the sunbonnet Emma grabbed up before the ride. When she and the Sansoms came back from hiding in the woods, Confederate soldiers were at the house with Turner's body. She did not say that Forrest was with them. She remembered that after the soldiers had gone, her mother and the Sansoms took food and water to a nearby spring where wounded Confederates had been left behind.[152]

Forrest's advance guard came over the creek quickly. It took perhaps two hours to get the main body across.

> *The cavalry went over, carrying by hand the ammunition from the caissons. The guns and empty caissons, with long ropes tied to the poles, were then rolled by hand to the water's edge, one end of the rope taken to the top of the opposite bank and hitched to double teams of horses. In this original manner the artillery soon made a subaqueous passage to the east bank. The advance guard had already hurried on after the raiders, who, to their great surprise, were hustled out of Gadsden.*[153]

Forrest had found a way over Black Creek.

Chapter 7
Surrender

Streight rode out of Gadsden for Rome on the Turkeytown Road, heading up the west bank of the Coosa River. He soon lost whatever lead he had gained at Black Creek. Forrest's advance guard was now beginning to pick up stragglers. Streight could not have known how Forrest got over Black Creek, but there he was, slashing at his rear again. Captain Smith was having a hard time fending them off. And as always, Streight was worried about that unidentified Confederate force off to his left; he was afraid that it might cut him off from Rome. It must have been clear to him that his only hope was to reach Rome with enough time to burn the bridge there over the Coosa River. He did not know about Emma Sansom, nor did he know that another Confederate civilian—"Georgia's Paul Revere"—was already riding to Rome to raise the alarm that the Yankees were coming.

"Georgia's Paul Revere" was John H. Wisdom, a mail carrier and ferryboat operator in Gadsden.[151] His mother lived in Rome, and he knew all the roads from Gadsden to Rome. On the morning of May 2, before Streight reached Gadsden, he had brought his buggy over the Coosa to deliver a sack of corn to a mill six miles to the east. He returned to Gadsden after Streight had left. His ferry had been burned. Three men on the far bank shouted to him that Yankee cavalry were on their way up the west bank, headed for Rome; they did not know that Forrest was chasing them. On the spot, Wisdom decided to warn Rome that they were coming. Over the next eleven or twelve hours, Wisdom outrode both Streight and Paul Revere, riding sixty-seven miles, beginning in his buggy, but also going through four horses and a mule, seven

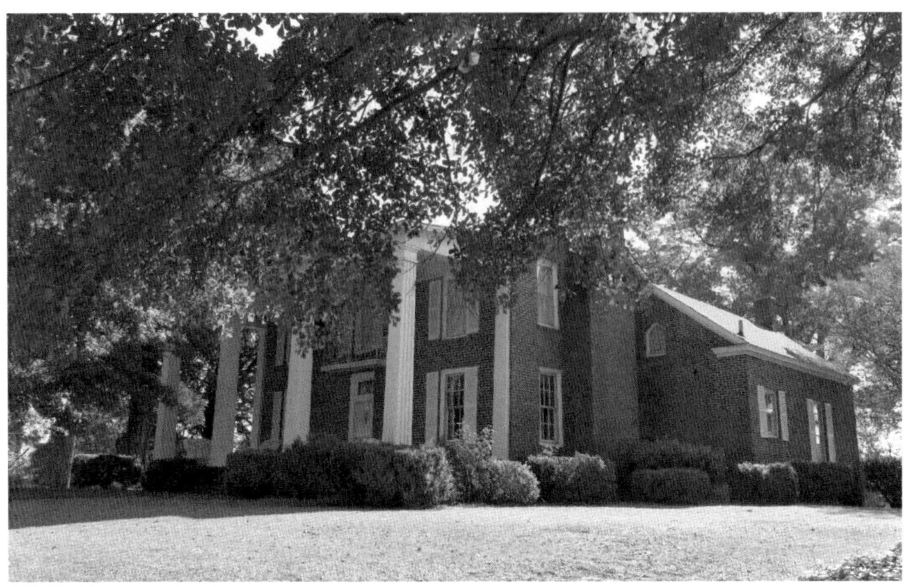

The Blount House, eight miles east of Gadsden on Route 411, which becomes Georgia Route 20 East. It is a beautifully restored "witness house" to the fight on May 2, 1863, and to the death and burial of Colonel Hathaway, 73rd Indiana. *Bob Price, photographer.*

hours by day and five by night. He reached Rome just before midnight on May 3. He reined in at the Etowah House, whose proprietor, George Black, was the local militia commander. Black immediately called out his militia, but John Wisdom went to his mother's house and fell asleep. As church bells tolled, Black organized his militia. "Within thirty minutes after his arrival, John Wisdom was probably the only man asleep in Rome."[155] (For more on Wisdom and Rome, see Appendix A.)

Streight, meantime, had covered about eight miles by 5:00 p.m., passing Turkeytown, nearing the Blount House, or plantation, on the Rome Road. "Here I decided to halt, as it was impossible to continue the march through the night without Feeding and resting."[156]

Rest—even a brief halt—was an absolute necessity, since they were facing an all-night trek to Rome. But the terrain west of the Blount House, along both sides of the main road, offered an opportunity to lay an ambush larger and more dangerous than those east of Hog Mountain.[157] Here, just east of the Croft House, the Rome Road begins a sharp descent. Coming downhill, the road was dominated by a ridge on its north side. That ridge sheltered a road running behind it, down to its intersection with the Rome Road. After crossing the Rome Road, it continued along high ground and a fence line south of the Rome Road.

Streight and Hathaway posted Company G of the 73rd Indiana just beyond the Croft House—bait for the oncoming Confederates. The rest of the regiment was at the bottom of the hill, at the four-way crossing. The 3rd Ohio and the 80th Illinois were on the ridge road, looking down on the Rome Road from the north. The 51st Indiana, and the two howitzers, now under Major Vananda, went into position along the fence line south of the intersection. Hathaway stayed near the two guns. If Forrest's main body, now no more than six hundred men, rode downhill, en masse, from the Croft House, they would ride into a trap more murderous than at Day's Gap. They would be taking plunging rifle and artillery fire from three sides.

But Forrest was careful. Since Day's Gap, he had been pursuing "in relays," resting as many of his men as he could while keeping smaller groups on Streight's rear. Forrest's men were "strung out," rather than bunched up. Men from the 9th Tennessee were in the lead with Ferrell's guns next. When the Federals fired, Ferrell's guns were still on level ground. They unlimbered and opened fire immediately. Men from the 4th Tennessee came downhill cautiously, extending their line to the right (south). Soon they had gone far enough to open enfilade fire on the 51st Indiana and the howitzers. Private Joseph Martin shot and killed Hathaway.[158] But even worse for Streight was the discovery that the dunking of the mules' packs at Wills Creek had soaked most of the ammunition. "Nearly all our remaining ammunition was worthless."[159] The discovery left him with no choice but to pull back a half-mile to a ridge east of the Blount House.

Union casualties for the engagement were not reported, but they were greater than Forrest's two killed and six wounded. Some of Colonel Hathaway's comrades asked the owner of the Blount House to bury him. Lacking a coffin or even planks to hammer together into a box, he buried the colonel in an oilcloth, carefully noting the grave site. In 1866, his wife recovered his body for reburial in Indianapolis.[160]

With Hathaway killed; ammunition ruined; men, horses, and mules bone-tired; many miles to Rome; and pursued by a foe he could neither defeat nor elude, could the situation have been worse? A Confederate prisoner now added more bad news, confirming Streight's belief that he didn't have nearly enough men to cope with Forrest. Sergeant "Parson" Haynes, a prisoner from the 4th Tennessee, gave Streight a wildly exaggerated estimate of Forrest's numbers. He said later that when he finished his fanciful account, Colonel Streight sighed and said, "Then they have got me."[161]

But Streight was not close to giving up. He intended to push on through the night. It was his third consecutive night march. He had to cross several small streams and then the Chattooga River before he reached the Coosa River at Rome. This night would be the most difficult night of all. He had only one other card to play. He ordered Captain Milton Russell of the 51st Indiana "to take 200 of his best mounted men from the whole command and proceed to Rome, and hold the bridge until the whole command could come up."[162] Russell left right away, but his mission was hopeless. He found a ferry across the Chattooga River, but only half his command was able to reach Rome. A soldier in the 80th Illinois wrote that "the other 100 had fallen by the way, their horses just falling in the road, the rest of us just ran over them in the road and left them."[163]

Those remaining with Streight pushed on, many riders asleep on their plodding animals. If Streight intended to cross the Coosa and go by way of Centre, on the east bank of the river, he did not. He learned that there was a Confederate force at Centre, so he continued on the west bank, passing Leesburg and then crossing Yellow Creek and Little River.

After about fifteen terrible miles, Streight reached Gee's Ferry on the Chattooga River, where Russell had crossed. But there was no ferry. It was gone. There was no bridge closer than Dykes' Bridge, near Gaylesville, about eight miles upstream. The road now led through a nightmarish country, which loggers had cleared to feed the furnaces of the local ironworks, the Cornwall and Round Mountain Furnaces.

Company A of the 3rd Ohio did some damage to the Round Mountain ironworks. But the road had become "a blackened endless series of wagon roads, leading off in all directions...open charred ground, with little attention to a road of any kind."[164] Companies drifted away from one another, men sleeping as they rode. Streight must have single-handedly kept different columns moving in generally the right direction. They finally reached Dykes' Bridge just before light on May 3. After crossing, they moved through Cedar Bluff, heading east for about two and a half miles before halting at the Lawrence House.

When Forrest found that at least the planks of Dykes' Bridge had been burned, he sent his men across the river on foot, some men leading horses, others holding rifles and cartridge boxes high overhead.[165] Whitsitt remembered: "Though the stream was swollen, we were ordered to plunge in and we got across by swimming a few yards in the middle of it. There was a deal of trouble about the cannon, but they were finally pulled across, while the ammunition was transported by means of canoes that the citizens provided."[166]

Forrest, with fewer than six hundred men, was now closing in. "There was now no more chance of getting away from Forrest than there was hope for the sea and shore to part."[167]

There would be no good news from Rome. Russell had arrived there at about 9:00 a.m. and found Rome ready for Streight. George Black had quickly spread Wisdom's news of the Federals' approach. Some people panicked, and a crowd formed at the Rome Railroad depot, hoping to flee to Kingston. But militia officers gathered their troops, old men and young boys, and marched them to the bridges or to the high ground overlooking town. Lieutenant H.C. Hooper from the Army of Northern Virginia, in Rome on a recruiting mission, helped organize the defense.[168] Convalescent soldiers came out and joined the militia. The bridges over the Etowah and Catoosa were barricaded and primed to burn. The Rome Railroad did its part; conductor C.A. Smith ran a train in from Kingston, carrying several hundred armed civilians. "We need more men," he wrote hastily to a friend. "If Forrest fails to catch them, then good-bye Rome."[169] From what Russell could see from Shorter's Hill, and from what several civilians told him, he decided he was too late to seize the Coosa bridge. He sent a courier dashing back to Streight and then turned his men back to the west.

It wouldn't have mattered if Russell and his hundred men had been able to take the bridge. Streight was at the end of his rope. His men could endure no more. Garfield's order—"Make the surrender of your command cost the enemy as many times your number as possible"—was an irrelevancy written in the world of staff officers and aides-de-camp. Soon after the halt near the Lawrence House, Streight's pickets came in—with no exchange of fire—saying that Forrest was only a few hundred yards away to the west. Wearily, Streight ordered his men into line of battle but found that "a large portion of my best troops actually went to sleep lying in line of battle."

But there was no shooting and no attack. Instead, Forrest sent Captain Henry Pointer riding slowly forward under a white flag of truce, proposing surrender.

Streight conferred with his officers; they were all for surrendering. He was still less willing to surrender than his regimental commanders, but after meeting with them a second time, he concluded that since he was hopelessly outnumbered, he had to give up. He wrote, "I yielded to the unanimous view of my regimental commanders and at once entered into negotiations with Forrest."[170] Whitsitt remembered Forrest saying earlier, "If he ever talks to me, then I've got him."[171]

Did Forrest bluff Streight into surrender by disguising and magnifying the size of his force? Forrest later said that Streight demanded that Forrest prove to him that his force, Forrest's, was far larger than his.[172] The story has been heavily embellished over the years. For example, the famous nineteenth-century Southern humorist known as Bill Arp (Charles Henry Smith, 1826–1903) explained that Forrest and Streight met under a cedar tree. Forrest bluffed Streight into surrender, which is how Cedar Bluff, Alabama, got its name.[173] That aside, there was certainly some Rebel play acting, and it went "without flaw."[174]

Forrest's men were hidden from view, but as the parley between the lines began, Lieutenant R.Y. Jones came into view with one of Forrest's two guns. "I was riding a little in advance of the gun, when suddenly looking up I saw General Forrest, Captain Pointer, one or two other officers, and several Federal officers sitting down on the north side of the road," Jones wrote.[175] Streight probably protested that Jones was violating the truce. Forrest would have told Pointer to move Jones back. A prominent knoll, on the north side to the road behind Forrest, gave the Confederates an excellent "stage prop" for moving guns and men into and out of Streight's clear view. It would have been a discouraging sight. According to one plausible story, Streight interjected at one point, "How many guns do you have? That's fifteen I've counted already!" Forrest replied, "I reckon that's all as has kept up."[176]

By about noon, Streight agreed to surrender about 1,450 men. He later reported 15 officers and 130 men killed and wounded and 200 men captured.[177] According to the terms, for the moment, his four regiments retained their colors, the officers retained their side arms, and officers and men retained their personal property. Within ten days, officers and men were to be paroled and sent to Virginia to be exchanged. As we will see, the officers would face a very different fate.[178]

There was one additional question, and it was dangerous. Streight requested that his men be allowed to "stack arms," i.e., march in formation with colors to an open field where they would formally relinquish (stack) their weapons. A site had to be found and Forrest's men would have to come out into the open, running the risk of revealing his true numbers. It was a tense situation. The Federals were marched down a "lane with immense fields of growing cotton on each side. That was the longest lane I have ever traveled," remembered Whitsitt. "It seemed like ten miles…Streight had almost 1,450 men and we had about 475 men in line…drawn up on both sides of them and every man of them [the prisoners] carried a loaded rifle and some likewise loaded pistols. If they had concluded to renew the struggle it is difficult to understand how any of us could have escaped alive."[179] Forrest played his part to perfection,

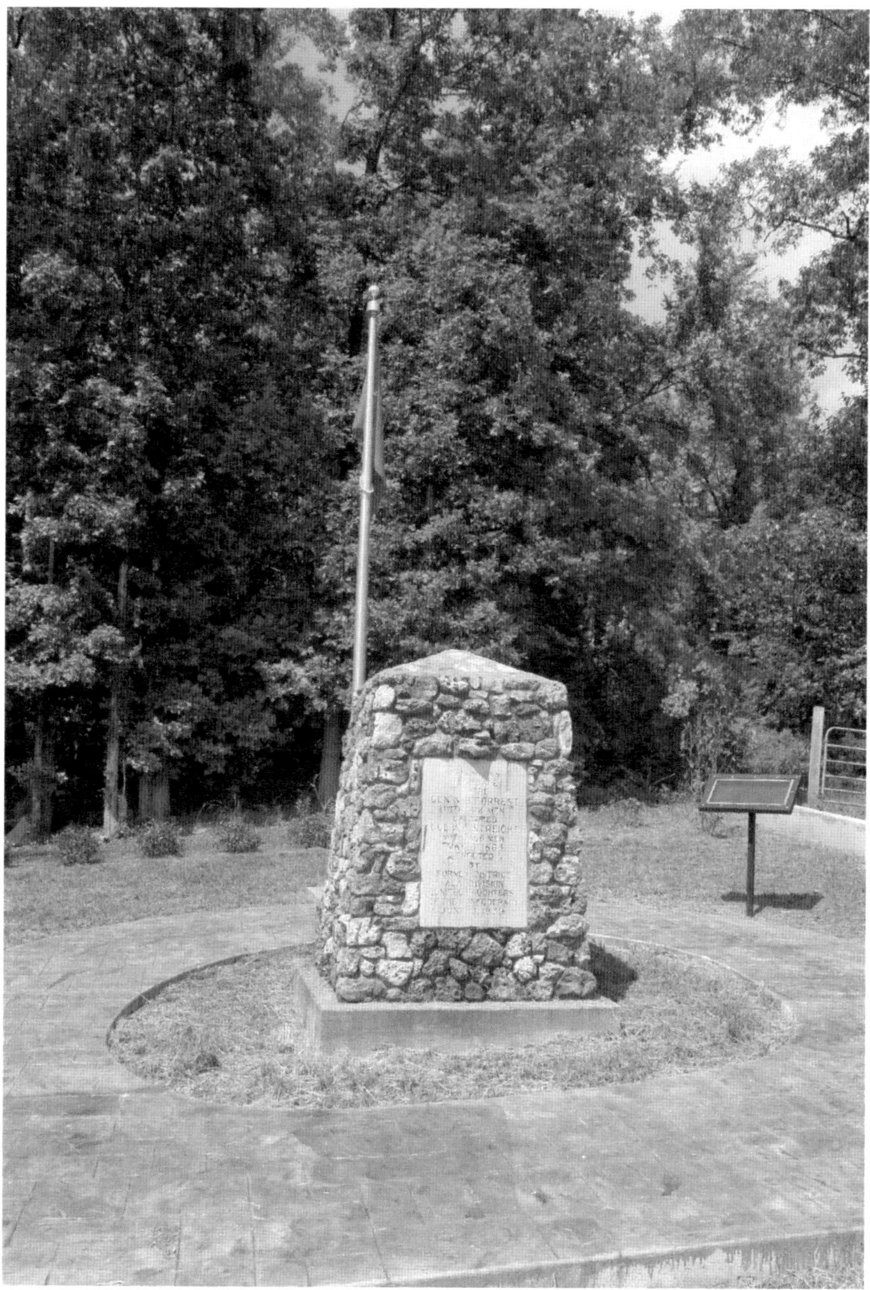

The Forney District of the United Daughters of the Confederacy unveiled this monument on June 3, 1939. There are historical markers on the site. The knoll that lent itself to the "play acting" of moving troops around, which confirmed Streight's belief that he was outnumbered, is just to the left (or west). *Bob Price, photographer.*

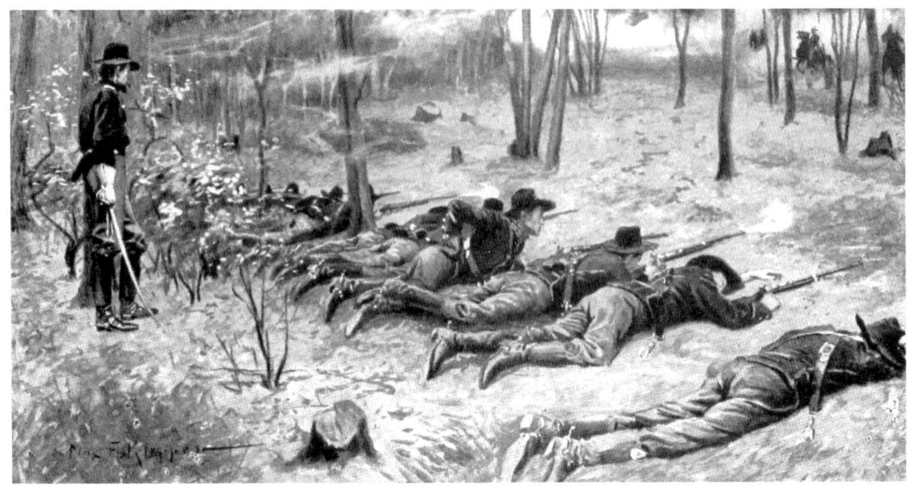

The last stand of Streight's raiders.

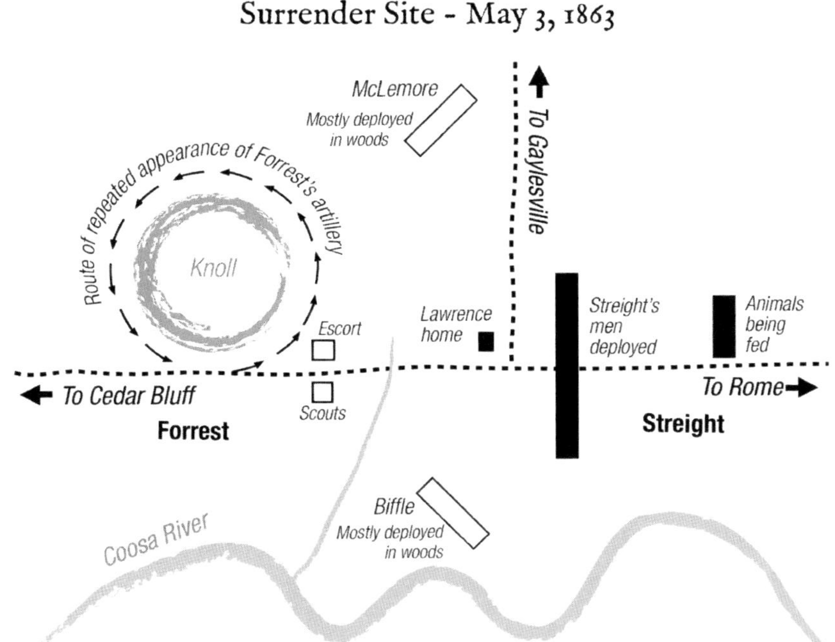

riding up and down, loudly sending out couriers with orders to bring in nearby troops immediately. There were no nearby troops.

Once the ceremony was completed, a vastly relieved Forrest left immediately for Rome, leaving Biffle in command. Russell's men surrendered without incident. Biffle separated the enlisted men from their officers and marched them on to Rome.

Colonel Robert Benjamin Kyle, an officer and quartermaster in the 31st Alabama Volunteer Infantry, traveled from his home in Gadsden to Rome that day. He recalled that Streight and most of his officers were enraged at having surrendered to a force they now knew was much smaller than theirs. They talked heatedly, Kyle wrote, of breaking out of captivity by sheer force of numbers. In response, guards tied up the most vocal officers, including Streight. When Kyle saw Streight, he was tied to a chair.[180] From Rome, the prisoners were sent east to Kingston and then on the W&A south to Atlanta. Officers and men were then sent north to separate destinations. The men were sent to City Point, Virginia, for exchange, and Streight and the officers were sent to Libby Prison in Richmond.

Things did not go so smoothly for either the officers or the Alabamians with Streight. Although all of them were in uniform, and their units were officially designated as Tennessee regiments, it was hard to forget the fate of eight of Andrews' raiders. Emotions ran high. For example, the *Jacksonville (AL) Republican* declared, "Let every mother's son of the 200 tory Alabamians be hung…without the benefit of clergy, as a partial punishment for the enormity of their crime and a wholesome lesson to all future traitors."[181] The day before, Governor John Gill Shorter of Alabama wrote to Confederate secretary of war James Seddon. Shorter claimed that the captured Alabamians were not ordinary prisoners of war but were, in fact, criminals who should be tried in civil courts in Alabama. They, he went on, were not only criminals in their state but also traitors to it.[182] Confederate authorities steered clear of what could have become a very bad situation. Seddon replied to Governor Shorter that all the men, including the Alabamians, had already been exchanged.[183]

The officers were not exchanged. The Confederate War Department informed Lieutenant Colonel William A. Ludlow, agent of exchange at Fort Monroe, that they were being held because of "offenses against the laws of [Alabama] and the usages of civilized warfare."[184]

The reference to "usages to civilized warfare" was a loaded one. Governor Shorter had also asked Secretary Seddon to determine from Forrest's report whether or not large numbers of slaves had been captured with Streight. Seddon assured him that there were none.[185]

Forrest later summed up the matters of the damage inflicted on civilian property and the slave question. He wrote, "Colonel Streight's command had done but little damage to property, having destroyed only one furnace and one stable." He did note that, especially at the end of the chase, the roadside was littered with items the raiders had stolen but had then cast off. Forrest went on to explain that many slaves had attached themselves to Streight's column, but most had escaped and returned to their masters. There were no more than fifteen with Streight at the time of the surrender, and none was armed.[186]

On February 9, 1864, 109 Union officers, including Streight, tunneled their way out of Libby Prison. Streight reported for duty soon afterward. He first returned to his regiment, and then later he took command of a brigade in the Army of the Cumberland for the rest of the War.[187]

The sense of relief in Rome was intense. Bill Arp, who had lived in Rome before the War, wrote in 1866 that "bouquets and tears were mixed up promiscuous...General Forrest subsided and General Jubilee took command."[188] Rome planned a barbeque for Forrest and his men on May 6, but orders came to Forrest late on May 5 to return west, to guard against another Union advance from Corinth. Orders then came to Forrest to send the command to Spring Hill and report to General Bragg at Shelbyville.[189]

For Alabama, Georgia, and the city of Rome, the surrender seemed like a providential deliverance—"a blessing from Almighty God," wrote one citizen.[190] The *Jacksonville Republican* headlined its page about the surrender in typical fashion: "Rome Threatened...Private Property Destroyed...200 Recreant Alabamians!!...1520 Federals Captured!... Great Excitement and Rejoicing."[191]

On May 6, Bragg telegraphed Governor Shorter, telling him that in a "bold and brilliant movement, Forrest, with half their number, pursued rapidly and fought them running for five days without forage or food except what he could hastily gather."[192] On May 28, Governor Joseph E. Brown issued a proclamation praising "gallant Forrest and his brave followers [who] stopped the destruction by the capture of the vandal force." Governor Brown called for "old men and young men to rally around the banner of their glorious old state and strike for their loved ones, their homes, their friends, and their altars."[193]

Atlanta, however, was alarmed that Streight had come as close as he had. "Indeed, it was Streight's raid that jarred Atlantans into realizing that the time had come for serious measures to protect their city from Union soldiers from the outside, not merely secret Yankees inside."

One such measure was the formation of the "Independent State Road Guards," made up of W&A railroaders. William C. Fuller was captain.[194]

Thanks to John Wisdom, Rome had rallied in its own defense. The grateful city gave him a cash award and a silver service set. The city also reimbursed Nancy Hanks of Gnatville, who had loaned Wisdom a pony. Citizens raised money to buy Forrest a fine horse. The company of old men and young boys that Lieutenant Hooper organized—six of whom were over forty-five and twenty under eighteen—"found favor with Forrest" and rode with him until the end of the War.[195]

Forrest spent the night of the seventh at Colonel Kyle's house in Gadsden. Forrest and Kyle's two-year-old son, Robert, took an instant liking to each other, and Forrest carried the boy around the house with him. The following morning, Colonel Kyle rode out of town with Forrest for two or three miles. The little boy rode with the general, sitting in front of him. When they parted, Forrest handed Robert over to his father, exclaiming, "My God, Kyle, this is worth living for."[196]

Kyle outlived Forrest, who died in 1877, and Streight, who died in 1892. At some point after the War, Kyle's business (lumber) took him to Indianapolis. Out walking, he saw a sign for "W.D. [*sic*] Streight, Lumber." On impulse, he decided to go in and reintroduce himself to Streight, whom he had last seen tied to a chair in Rome, Georgia. They had a friendly conversation, about what, Kyle did not say. He did note that Streight was still angry over the "military trickery" that he said led him to surrender.[197]

Afterword

The two raids on the W&A were courageously carried out but almost certainly destined to fail. In the end, Andrews could not escape the determined pursuit of William Fuller, and Streight could not escape Forrest.

Andrews' strike had been sudden, even if a day late. Streight, on the other hand, needed twenty-three days merely to get into position to begin his raid. Poorly mounted and endlessly tormented by Forrest's pursuit, he was Forrest's prisoner a week after he set out. Even if he had defeated Forrest or succeeded in putting the Coosa River between his force and the Confederates, it is difficult to see how a worn-down force of infantry, with no tools, was going to be able to do significant damage to a guarded, important railroad. And even if he had, there was no realistic chance to escape. Andrews was at least fleeing toward an approaching Union force. Streight was not.

The big picture from across the Confederacy, however, tells a much different story. Grant's march down the west bank of the Mississippi was successful. On April 30, he crossed the river south of Vicksburg. The cavalry diversions—Grierson's and, to a lesser extent, Streight's—had worked.

Theater commander Joseph E. Johnston's decision in January to bring Van Dorn's cavalry from Mississippi and combine his force with Forrest's south of Nashville had served Bragg and the Army of Tennessee well. But Johnston still faced a harsh strategic dilemma. He had to choose between Mississippi, on the one hand, and Tennessee and Alabama, on the other. Moving Van Dorn left Pemberton dangerously vulnerable. Not moving Van Dorn would have left Bragg dangerously vulnerable. Writing to his brother

Joseph on May 7, 1863, before he learned of Van Dorn's death that day, President Jefferson Davis lamented, "The withdrawal of Van Dorn from North Mississippi is one of those blunders which it is difficult to compensate for."[198]

The Confederate Congress voted its thanks to Forrest for his brilliant success in North Alabama.[199] But the victory was eclipsed as Grant began applying his stranglehold on Vicksburg.

The president went on to say of Van Dorn, "A general in the full acceptance of the word is a rare product...Scarcely more than one can be expected in a generation...There is need now for a half dozen."[200]

But on the day Davis wrote those words, a jealous husband killed Van Dorn in his headquarters at Spring Hill, Tennessee. Three days later, Stonewall Jackson died at Guinea Station, in Virginia. When Reverend Whitsitt learned of Jackson's death, he wrote, "I can never forget the sorrow and foreboding."[201] Forrest succeeded Van Dorn and became the greatest cavalryman of the War. But who could succeed Jackson?

The W&A survived Andrews, and it survived Streight. But it could not survive the loss of Chattanooga. The fall of Chattanooga in early September 1863 opened the avenue of invasion—down the line of the W&A—to Atlanta. By May 1864, the W&A was, in effect, two railroads, one supplying Sherman, southbound from Chattanooga, and the other shrinking as Johnston fell back below the Chattahoochee.

For many people, the most memorable scene in *Gone With the Wind* is of the hundreds or even thousands of wounded Confederate soldiers lying in the foreground of the W&A train shed in Atlanta. It was the last W&A station still in Confederate hands. The wounded men are waiting for trains south into what remained of the Confederacy.

Appendix A

John Wisdom: Georgia's Paul Revere

John Wisdom has come down to us as Georgia's Paul Revere. As a ferryboat operator and mail carrier in the Coosa River Valley, Wisdom, whose mother lived in Rome, instinctively felt the need to help and warn his neighbors. He knew them well, and he knew the roads that linked them together.

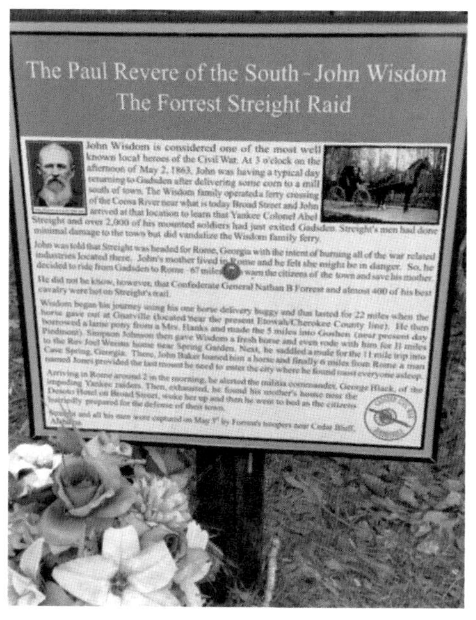

John Wisdom marker, at his grave in Hoke's Bluff, Alabama. *Melissa W. Beck, photographer.*

Wisdom's ride would have been impossible for anyone without his knowledge of the country between Gadsden and Rome. He covered the first twenty-two miles in his buggy from Gadsden, by way of Hoke's Bluff to Gnatville. Looking for a fresh horse, he could find only a lame pony, loaned to him by Nancy Hanks. At sunset, five miles farther on, at Goshen, "Simps" Johnson loaned him a fresh horse and rode with him for eleven miles to the Reverend Allen Whem's house on the road from Jacksonville and Blue Mountain to Rome. Whem had a pair of mules, and the two men went on for eleven more miles to John Baker's house, a mile west of Cave Spring. Baker loaned him a fresh horse for the ride to the house of a man named Jones, six miles south of Rome. From there, Wisdom rode into Rome, stopping at the

Etowah House to give the news to militia commander George Black, and from there to his mother's house.

From late afternoon of May 2 to midnight, Wisdom rode sixty-five miles in eleven hours, using four horses and one mule—each, according to Wisdom, "rougher riding than the last one." [202]

John Wisdom died on July 20, 1909, and is buried in the Hoke's Bluff Baptist Cemetery in Hoke's Bluff, Alabama.

Appendix B

Emma Sansom's Legacy

Emma Sansom was born in Social Circle, Georgia, on June 2, 1847. A historical marker installed there in 1928 commemorates her birth. She was the last of thirteen children born to Micajah and Lamila Vann Sansom. The family moved to Gadsden in 1852, and her father farmed on the west bank of Black Creek until his death in 1859. He is buried in the small family cemetery now in the median of Meighan Boulevard in Gadsden. Emma and her sister Mary Jane (Jennie) stayed on with their mother after their father's death. Emma was a member of the Missionary Baptist Church in Gadsden. Five of her six brothers were Confederate soldiers. William, Rufus, and Orren served in the 19th Alabama. John was in the 36th Georgia, and J.L. "Joe" was in the 16th Texas Cavalry. Miraculously, they all survived the War.

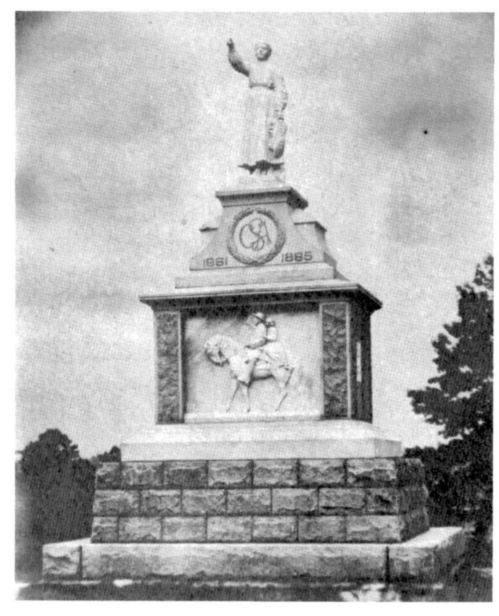

The Emma Sansom story made front-page news in the *Gadsden Daily News-Times*, July 4, 1907. *Danny Crownover, Etowah County Historical Society.*

Emma's life changed rapidly soon after she "showed Forrest the way." Her fame spread quickly. As early as May 9, the *Jacksonville Republican* saluted her as a "true heroine." (The *Republican* got her name wrong. Its article saluted "Jane Sanson.") In November 1863, the Alabama legislature voted to award her a gold medal and 640 acres of land for her heroism at Black Creek. Despite a public ceremony announcing the award, it was never made. In 1864, she married Christopher Bullard Johnson from Cherokee County, Alabama. He was thirty-two, and she was seventeen. He was a veteran of the 10th Alabama who served until suffering a crippling leg wound at the Battle of Gaines Mill in Virginia. They had eight children. The first, Mattie Forrest, died in 1871; she, too, is buried in the small family cemetery. But the survival of Emma's brothers and seven of her children ensured that the family line and legacy would survive down to the present. Emma's great-grandson Larry Johnson is the keeper of the family flame and, fittingly, Emma and Christopher's family Bible.

Johnson owned land in Texas, and the couple began moving there in 1876. He left first, leaving Emma to sell some lots in Gadsden. Emma wrote to Christopher on July 2, 1876. She said that she was "tired of living in one state and you in another and you may rest assured that if I follow you to Texas that you will never get one days journey from me again as long as I live. Write often and I will come as soon as I can."[203] She was able to sell the land, but for some unexplained reason, she was never paid. The couple lived in Callaway, Texas, now Little Mound, in Upshur County. Christopher died in 1887, leaving Emma, then forty, to raise seven children between the ages of two and nineteen. Emma's mother, Lamila, died in 1895.

In March 1896, Emma made her second great contribution to the history of the War; she responded to a letter from Dr. John Allan Wyeth, who was then working on his great biography of Forrest, *Life of Lieutenant General Nathan Bedford Forrest*. Dr. Wyeth asked her to review his account of what had happened on May 2, 1863, and to send him her photograph. She wrote a memoir of the day at Black Creek. It was the only time in her life that she drew attention to herself for what she had done. Wyeth's book was published three years later, in 1899.

Emma did not seek to capitalize on her heroism at Black Creek, but others recognized the importance of what she had done. The United Confederate Veterans invited her to their reunion in Birmingham in 1893 and in Atlanta in 1898. She attended both, and she was awarded a Forrest Cavalry Corps medal, as an honorary member of Forrest's cavalry.

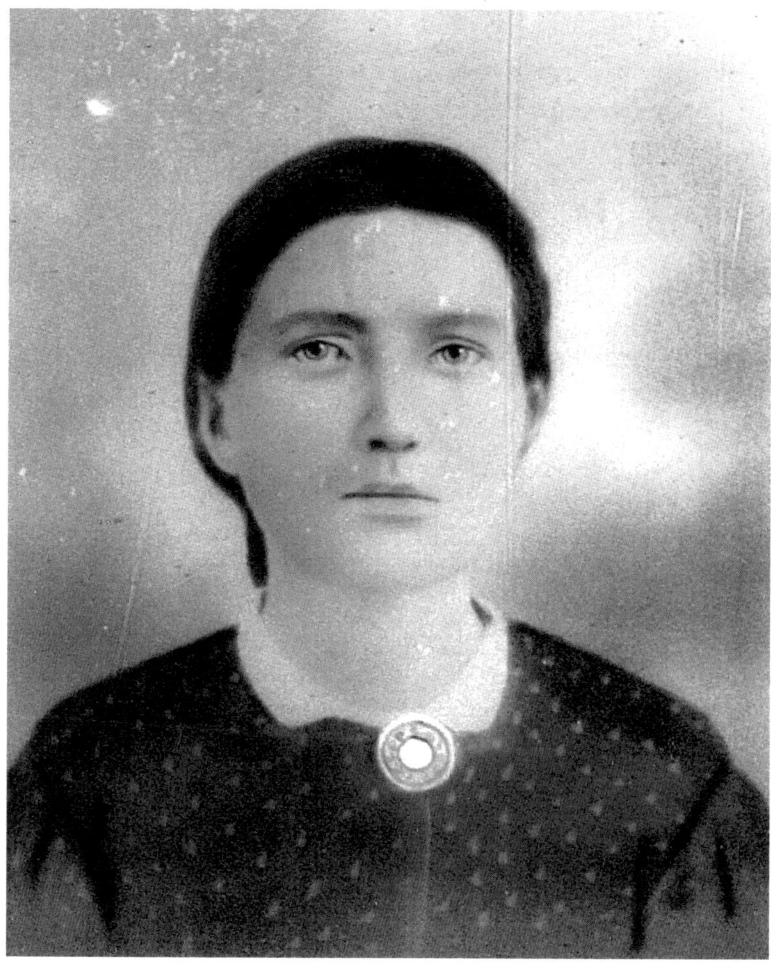

A picture of Emma later in life, from Mary Nell James, Emma's great-granddaughter, and Larry Johnson, her great-grandson. *Larry Johnson, personal collection.*

In 1899, the Alabama legislature tried to make good its promise from 1863, voting seventy-seven to five to award her a section of land. However, Emma declined; she was comfortably situated in Upshur County, surrounded by children and grandchildren. She also suffered from consumption (tuberculosis) and died in 1900. She is buried in the Little Mound Baptist Church Cemetery, next to Christopher. Her legacy is founded on more than just showing Forrest the way. She lived a life of duty, devotion, and hard work. She was a support for her widowed mother, her handicapped husband, and her young children, whom she raised alone. She made a mark on history and gave her only account of it to a great historian, Dr. John Wyeth. Her life is remembered in historical markers at her birthplace in Georgia and her grave in Texas. There is a marker at the family cemetery in Gadsden and a pink Texas granite monument in the courthouse square in Gilmer, Texas, the county seat of Upshur County.

She was the subject of at least thirty different articles in *Confederate Veteran*, the magazine of the United Confederate Veterans, now the Sons of Confederate Veterans. Many United Daughters of the Confederacy chapters and United Confederate Veterans camps adopted her name:

- The Emma Sansom Camp of the United Confederate Veterans, Gadsden, 1893
- The Emma Sansom Chapter 449 of the United Daughters of the Confederacy, Santa Ana, California, 1899
- The Emma Sansom Chapter 2654 of the United Daughters of the Confederacy, Rome, Georgia
- The Emma Sansom Chapter Order of the Confederate Rose, De Ridder, Louisiana
- The Emma Sansom Chapter Order of the Confederate Rose, Tyler, Texas
- The Emma Sansom Chapter 2701 of the United Daughters of the Confederacy, Gilmer, Texas, 2014

It is in Gadsden, of course, that her legacy is most deeply felt. The Emma Sansom Middle School, formerly High School, on Meighan Boulevard, is the site of the Sansom farmhouse—it actually stood at the southeast corner of the gym. The cemetery in the Meighan Boulevard median is almost directly across from the home site. Running parallel with Meighan Boulevard on its north side is Tuscaloosa Avenue, the Old Tuscaloosa Road. It crosses Black Creek at the site of the bridge that Streight burned. The low water ford that Emma Sansom showed Forrest is two hundred yards north upstream.

The whereabouts of the note General Forrest left on the bureau of the Sansom house are unknown. Emma presented Dr. Wyeth the original note. He published a facsimile of it in his biography, published in 1899 and again in 1908, between pages 212 and 213. The note may have been lost in a fire, perhaps, in Dr. Wyeth's New York office. If so, the facsimile is all that we will ever have. But Dr. Wyeth dedicated the biography to Emma in gratitude for helping him and for helping Forrest. The dedication reads:

To Emma Sansom
A woman worthy of being remembered
by her countrymen as long as courage is deemed a virtue,
who rode with General Forrest,
in the engagement at Black Creek May 2, 1863,
and by guiding his men to an unguarded ford
enabled him to capture Colonel A.D. Streight
and his entire command,
this volume is dedicated
as a token of admiration and respect.

Memphis, Forrest's virtual hometown, was the scene of the Forrest Cavalry reunion in October 1906. Veterans rode on parade through downtown Memphis, with a riderless horse in memory of Emma's ride with Forrest.[204]

Finally, a fine life-sized statue of Emma looks out over Gadsden from the west end of Broad Street, at the foot of the modern bridge over the Coosa River. The Gadsden chapter of the United Daughters of the Confederacy unveiled the statue on July 4, 1907. The *Gadsden Times-News* recorded the event: "When the cloth dropped, exposing the pure white shaft to the brilliant light of the noonday sun, the great throng indulged in deafening and prolonged shouts and cheers. Patriotic songs and recitations filled the remainder of the program."

The statue is depicted on the city seal: Emma showing the way.

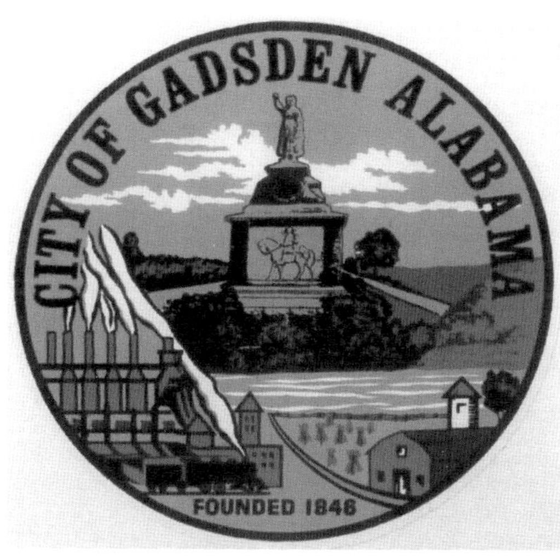

The Gadsden, Alabama city seal, 2015. *Danny Crownover and Larry Johnson.*

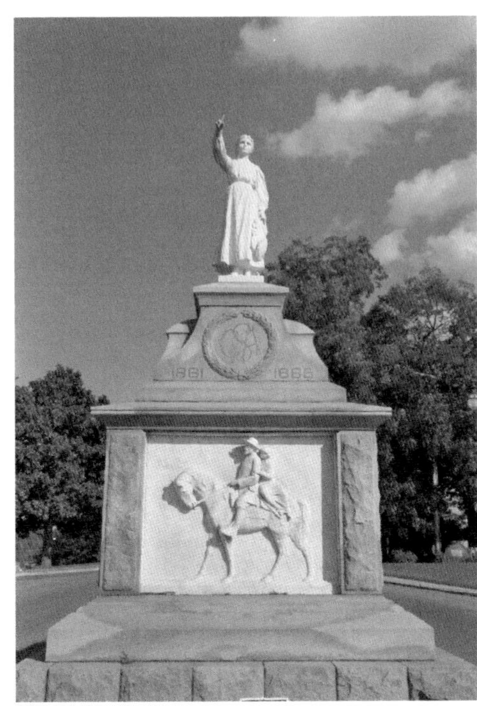

Emma Sansom showing Forrest the way, at Gadsden, Alabama. *Bob Price, photographer.*

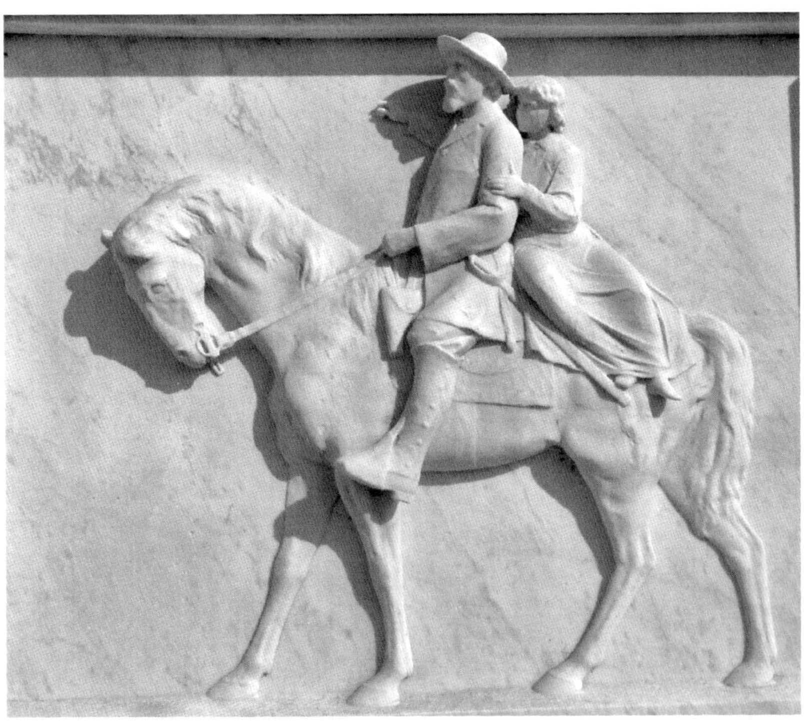

Notes

Chapter 1

1. Cleveland, *Alexander H. Stephens*, 605–11.
2. Garrison, *Atlanta and the War*, 18–21.
3. The present location of the Zero Milepost is "on the interior wall of the Georgia Building Authority's headquarters, on the first floor of the parking garage, immediately adjacent to the southern entrance to underground Atlanta. Enter the main entrance of the parking garage from Central Avenue, and ride an elevator down to the first floor. Enter the Georgia Building Authority's headquarters and you'll find a historical marker mounted on a wall next to the Zero Milepost. Knock or wave, and someone will open the door for you during normal business hours, Monday–Friday." From "Western & Atlantic Zero Milepost," http://www.nps.gov/nr/travel/atlanta/wes.htm.
4. Bogle, "Civil War Railroads," 33. See also Phillips, "An American State-Owned Railroad," 259–70, and Gates, "Notes and Documents," 169–84.
5. "W&A Railroad Tunnel," http://www.tunnelhillheritagecenter.com; "Western & Atlantic Railroad," http://www.ourgeorgiahistory.com. See also Bogle, "Civil War Railroads," 30–31.
6. Bryan, "Chattanooga," 291. See also Wilson, "Chattanooga Railroad Series."
7. Bonds, *Stealing the General*, 151.
8. Johnston, *Western and Atlantic Railroad*, 49–50, 65. See also "Western and Atlantic Railroad," http://www.georgia.com.

9. Gates, "Impact of the Western & Atlantic Railroad," 172–73.
10. Bonds, *Stealing the General*, 92.
11. Garrison, *Atlanta and the War*, 21.
12. Russell, *Atlanta 1847–1890*, 46, 102.
13. Garrison, *Atlanta and the War*, 23.
14. Bonds, *Stealing the General*, 75. See also Stover, "Railroads," 1,293–99.

Chapter 2

15. Cozzens, *Darkest Days of the War*, 25.
16. Bonds, *Stealing the General*, 28.
17. Buell, "Operations in North Alabama," 701.
18. Pittenger, "Locomotive Chase," 709–16. For the full story of the Andrews Raid, see Aiken, *The Great Locomotive Chase*. See also Bonds, *Stealing the General*, and Turner, *Victory Rode the Rails*, 166–77.
19. Pittenger, "Locomotive Chase," 709.
20. Bonds, *Stealing the General*, 46.
21. Pittenger, "Locomotive Chase," 710.
22. Ibid., 711.
23. For Kingston, see Jackson, *Tales of the Rails*, 18. For a good map of the Kingston trackwork, see Bonds, *Stealing the General*, 141.
24. Bonds, *Stealing the General*, 154.
25. Pittenger, "Locomotive Chase," 712; Bonds, *Stealing the General*, 154.
26. Bonds, *Stealing the General*, 147.
27. Pittenger, "Locomotive Chase," 711.
28. Ibid., 712.
29. Ibid., 713.
30. Turner, *Victory Rode the Rails*, 175.
31. Pittenger, "Locomotive Chase," 714.
32. For a complete description of Andrews' hanging, see Bonds' preface in *Stealing the General*.
33. Davis, *What the Yankees Did*, 54.
34. Hess, *Civil War in the West*, 92.
35. Daniel, *Days of Glory*, 102–3.
36. McWhiney, *Braxton Bragg*, 268.
37. Black, *Railroads of the Confederacy*, 180–84.
38. Black, "The Railroads of Georgia," 522.

Chapter 3

39. "51st Indiana Infantry in the American Civil War," http://www.civilwarindex.com, n.d.
40. Willett, *Lightning Mule Brigade*, 17–18.
41. Streight, *Crisis*, 50, 82–83.
42. Nowland, *Sketches of Prominent Citizens*, 502–6.
43. Danielson, *War's Desolating Scourge*, 77.
44. Storey, *Loyalty and Loss*, 2. See also Degler, "Unionism," 1,636–40.
45. Todd, *First Alabama Cavalry*, 4–5.
46. U.S. War Department, *War of the Rebellion* (henceforth cited as *O.R.*), ser. 1, vol. 16, 785–90.
47. Wills, *Battle from the Start*, 44.
48. Duncan, *Recollections*, 31.
49. Botkin, *Civil War Treasury*, 185.
50. Whitsitt, "A Year with Forrest," 357–62.
51. *O.R.*, ser. 1, vol. 52, part 2, 402. Also Jones, *Confederate Strategy*, 111–13.
52. Roland, *An American Iliad*, 121.
53. *O.R.*, ser. 1, vol. 17, part 2, 813. See also 832–33. Also see vol. 20, part 2, 898 and vol. 23, part 2, 646.
54. Ibid., vol. 20, part 2, 898.
55. Henry, *"First with the Most" Forrest*, 128.
56. *O.R.*, ser. 1, vol. 24, part 3, 686. Also ser. 1, vol. 52, part 2, 425.
57. "The Story of Roderick," http://www.RoderickPlace.com, n.d. See also Wyeth, *That Devil Forrest*, 141.
58. Witherspoon, "Confederate Cavalry Leaders," 416. See also Henry, *"First with the Most" Forrest*, 135.
59. Daniel, *Soldiering*, 57.
60. *O.R.*, ser. 1, vol. 20, part 2, 494.
61. Ibid., vol. 23, part 2, 625–26.
62. Black, *Railroads of the Confederacy*, 195.
63. For a general discussion on the logistical situation, see Daniel, *Soldiering in the Army of Tennessee*, 55–74. For a thorough discussion of Confederate supply in Virginia and Tennessee, see McMurry, *Two Great Rebel Armies*.

CHAPTER 4

64. Basler, *Collected Works of Abraham Lincoln*, 108.
65. Willett, *Lightning Mule Brigade*, 11, cites Streight's service record.
66. Lamers, *Edge of Glory*, 257.
67. I am indebted to Jim Woodrick, director of the Mississippi Department of Archives and History, for the unpublished manuscript by Warren E. Grabau, "'It Will Be a Terrible Blow': Streight's Raid Across North Alabama, 8 April–4 May, 1863," 2003, 2, 8–10. See also Bearss, "Streight Drives," 133–86.
68. *O.R.*, ser. 1, vol. 23, part 2, 214.
69. Grabau, "Terrible Blow," 42; Willett, *Lightning Mule Brigade*, 15, 23. See also Keith S. Hebert, "Streight's Raid," www.encyclopediaofalabama.org/article/h-1380.
70. Whitsitt, "A Year with Forrest," 359.
71. Willett, *Lightning Mule Brigade*, 21.
72. Grabau, "Terrible Blow," 42.
73. *O.R.*, ser. 1, vol. 23, part 1, 282.
74. Bearss, "Streight Drives," 133–35.
75. Williams, *Wild Life of the Army*, 258.
76. Cofield, "William Faulkner and the Mule Picture."
77. *O.R.*, ser. 1, vol. 23, part 1, 285. (Streight's report, August 22, 1864, 285–93, henceforth cited as "Streight report").
78. Armistead, *Horses and Mules*, 30.
79. Whitsitt, "A Year with Forrest," 359.
80. I am grateful to Dr. Jim Dowdle of the Columbus, Mississippi Animal Medical Center for this information.
81. Streight report, 285.
82. Stanton J. Brumfield letter to his wife, Mary Jane, April 20, 1863, Indiana Historical Society, Indianapolis, Indiana.
83. Ibid.
84. Bearss, "Streight Drives," 145; Willett, *Lightning Mule Brigade*, 37.
85. Brumfield letter.
86. Danielson, *War's Desolating Scourge*, 120, cites Thomas Hoffman's diary, State Historical Society of Iowa.
87. Willett, *Lightning Mule Brigade*, 17.
88. Streight report, 286.
89. Willett, *Lightning Mule Brigade*, 60–61.
90. McCash, "Colonel Abel D. Streight's Raid," 81.

91. Willett, *Lightning Mule Brigade*, 65, cites Committee of the Seventy-Third Indiana Regimental Association, *History of the Seventy-Third Indiana Volunteers*.
92. Streight report, 287.
93. *O.R.*, ser. 1, vol. 23, part 1, 282.
94. Bearss, "Streight Drives," 173.

Chapter 5

95. *O.R.*, ser. 1, vol. 23, part 2, 788.
96. Willett, *Lightning Mule Brigade*, 17.
97. Jordan and Pryor, *Campaigns of General Nathan Bedford Forrest*, 250–51.
98. Willett, *Lightning Mule Brigade*, 97.
99. Fulenwider, *Civil War Stories*, 1.
100. Streight report, 287; *O.R.*, ser. 1, vol. 23, part 1, 248.
101. *O.R.*, ser. 1, vol. 23, part 1, 249.
102. Ibid., part 2, 799; Dinkins, "Forrest's Pursuit" (December 1925), 452–54 and (January 1926), 15–16; Grabau, "Terrible Blow," 22.
103. Grabau, "Terrible Blow," 23.
104. Starnes, *Forrest's Forgotten Horse Brigadier*, 69; Fisher, *They Rode with Forrest*, 39.
105. John McKee diary, 2nd Iowa Infantry, 1863–1864, United States Army Heritage and Education Center, Carlisle, Pennsylvania.
106. Dinkins, "Pursuit and Capture," 452.
107. *O.R.*, ser. 1, vol. 23, part 2, 799.
108. Bearss, "Streight Drives," 157.
109. Rucker Agee letter, n.d., courtesy of Norwood Kerr, Mississippi Department of Archives and History, Montgomery, Alabama.
110. Ibid., 5.
111. For the names of Smith's men and their nearby relatives, see Fulenwider, *Civil War Stories*, 2.
112. Streight report, 287.
113. Wyeth, *That Devil Forrest*, 180; McCash, "Streight's Raid," 134; Jordan and Pryor, *Campaigns of Forrest*, 256–57.
114. Agee, "Forrest-Streight Campaign of 1863," 11.
115. Wyeth, *That Devil Forrest*, from W.G. Wilkins' diary in Wyeth's collection, 175–76.
116. Roach, *Prisoner of War*, 226.
117. Bearss, "Streight Drives," 168.

118. Whitsitt, "A Year with Forrest," 359.
119. Duncan, *Recollections*, 114–16.
120. Ibid. Forrest never forgave Gould for the loss of the guns—so much so that Gould, feeling that Forrest demeaned his courage and honor, tried to kill Forrest six weeks later in Columbia, Tennessee. He wounded Forrest severely, but Forrest then stabbed Gould, mortally wounding him.
121. Fulenwider, *Civil War Stories*, 3.
122. Jordan and Pryor, *Campaigns of Forrest*, 259.
123. McCash, "Streight's Raid," 149.
124. Willett, *Lightning Mule Brigade*, 112, 116, 173.
125. Whitsitt, "A Year with Forrest," 360.
126. Walsh, *Those Damn Horse Soldiers*, 136.
127. McCash, "Streight's Raid," 151–52.
128. Agee, "Forrest-Streight Campaign of 1863," 6.
129. Whitsitt, "A Year with Forrest," 360.
130. William Spencer memoir, "My Capture: Seven Months in Libby Prison," William Spencer collection (SC1387), Indiana Historical Society, Indianapolis, Indiana.
131. Willett, *Lightning Mule Brigade*, 176, 178.
132. Whitsitt, "A Year with Forrest," 360.
133. Wyeth, *That Devil Forrest*, 182.
134. Fulenwider, *Civil War Stories*, 5.
135. Blount County Historical Society, *Forrest-Streight Raid.*
136. Willett, *Lightning Mule Brigade*, 128, cites Committee of the Seventy-Third Indiana Regimental Association's *History of the Seventy-Third Indiana Volunteers*, 142–43.
137. Streight report, 290.
138. Willett, *Lightning Mule Brigade*, 129; Fulenwider, *Civil War Stories*, 5.
139. Brumfield letter.
140. Crownover, "Exploit of the Murphree Sisters," cites research by Laura D. Elliot. Also see Willett, *Lightning Mule Brigade*, 172. Arminda's husband, Isaac, was killed, as were two of their sons. Both sisters married after the war.
141. Bearss, "Streight Drives," 175–76.
142. Ibid., 128.
143. Agee, "Forrest-Streight Campaign of 1863," 6.
144. Crawford, "A Note on Forrest's Race for Rome," 288–90.

Chapter 6

145. Wyeth, *That Devil Forrest*, 186. Wyeth originally published the biography as *Life of Lieutenant General Nathan Bedford Forrest* (1899). See bibliography. In the 1908 edition, Wyeth's description of Black Creek is on pages 207–8.
146. Mary Harrison Lister collection, copy of a *Gadsden Times* article, November 26, 1939, Gadsden Public Library, Gadsden, Alabama.
147. Marshall, Smith, and Wren, *Alabama Collection Camps*, 253.
148. All of my information about Emma Sansom, except where noted otherwise, comes from her generous great-grandson Larry Johnson, of Arlington, Texas.
149. Wyeth, *That Devil Forrest*, 188–90. The account Emma gave to Dr. Wyeth is on pages 209–12 in the 1908 edition of the book published with the title *Life of Lieutenant General Nathan Bedford Forrest.* The facsimile of the note General Forrest left Emma is on an unnumbered page just prior to page 213.
150. This photograph of Forrest's note is from Larry Johnson's personal collection. Wyeth published a facsimile of the note in his *Life of Lieutenant General Nathan Bedford Forrest* (1899). Later editions of the biography include *That Devil Forrest* in the titles. There is a copy of the text of the note in Botkin's *Civil War Treasury*, 255–57. It was included in the Morningside edition, 1975, of Wyeth's biography. Emma probably gave Dr. Wyeth the original copy, which may have burned in a fire that destroyed Dr. Wyeth's office, perhaps in New York City.
151. *Gadsden Times*, August 17, 1958. Garrett's grandson R.N. Taylor, who lived in Gadsden, was the source of this account. In 1908, Garrett was elected vice-president of the Forrest Escort Association.
152. Lister collection, letter from Mrs. J.B. McKinnon, formerly Mary Blair, December 1, 1929.
153. Wyeth, *That Devil Forrest*, 190.

Chapter 7

154. For John Wisdom, see Aycock, "John Wisdom's Ride" and "Two Famous Rides Compared."
155. Aycock, "Georgia's Paul Revere." The author relied on an account of Wisdom's ride written in 1906 by J.M. Robertson, who knew Wisdom.
156. Streight report, 291.
157. I am indebted to Norman Dasinger Jr., of Gadsden, a guide with the Civil War Education Association, for his interpretation of the fight at the Blount House.

158. Willett, *Lightning Mule Brigade*, 148.
159. Streight report, 291.
160. Willett, *Lightning Mule Brigade*, 148–49, 172.
161. Dinkins, "Pursuit and Capture" (January 1926): 17.
162. Streight report, 291.
163. Willett, *Lightning Mule Brigade*, 150, citing James Lawson Brown journal, Loomis collection, Centralia, Illinois.
164. Glazner, *Geography*, 113, 161.
165. Willett, *Lightning Mule Brigade*, 162.
166. Whitsitt, "A Year with Forrest," 360–61.
167. Dinkins, "Pursuit and Capture," 17.
168. Battey, *History of Rome and Floyd County*, 192.
169. Willett, *Lightning Mule Brigade*, 158.
170. Streight report, 292.
171. Whitsitt, "A Year with Forrest," 361.
172. Willett, *Lightning Mule Brigade*, 164.
173. Arp, *Side Show*, 39.
174. Willett, *Lightning Mule Brigade*, 164.
175. Bearss, "Streight Drives," 184.
176. Fisher, *They Rode with Forrest and Wheeler*, 42.
177. Streight report, 293.
178. Willett, *Lightning Mule Brigade*, 164.
179. Whitsitt, "A Year with Forrest," 361.
180. Will Martin collection, Gadsden Public Library, February 21, 1947.
181. *Jacksonville (AL) Republican*, "Gen. Forrest in Rome," vol. 27, no. 17, May 9, 1863.
182. *O.R.*, ser. 2, vol. 5, 946–47.
183. Ibid., 956.
184. Ibid., 960.
185. Ibid., 969.
186. Ibid., vol. 6, 414.
187. Willett, *Lightning Mule Brigade*, 193–96.
188. Arp, *A Side Show*, 40.
189. Henry, *"First with the Most" Forrest*, 160–61.
190. Danielson, *War's Desolating Scourge*, 171.
191. *Jacksonville Republican*, "Gen. Forrest in Rome," May 9, 1863.
192. Bragg to Shorter, May 6, 1863, Southern Telegraph Co., Mississippi Department of Archives and History, Montgomery, Alabama.
193. Brown, *Confederate Records*, 447.

194. Davis, *What the Yankees Did*, 55–56.
195. "A Company Made Favor with Gen. Forrest," *Confederate Veteran* 22 (March 1914), 130–31.
196. Wyeth, *That Devil Forrest*, 199.
197. Will Martin collection, Gadsden Public Library, February 21, 1947.

Afterword

198. Cooper, *Jefferson Davis*, 301–2.
199. *O.R.*, ser. 1, vol. 23, part 1, 295.
200. Cooper, *Jefferson Davis*, 301–2.
201. Whitsitt, "A Year with Forrest," 361.

Appendix A

202. Aycock, "Georgia's Paul Revere."

Appendix B

203. Letter, Larry Johnson's collection.
204. Joseph A. Ricci, "Captain Dinkins in War and Peace," *Memorial Hall Foundation Newsletter* (Summer 2016), 5, cites the *New Orleans Times Picayune*, "Forrest's Cavalry to Meet Today. Dinkins Will Lead Riderless Horse in Memory of 'Girl Hero,'" (October 17, 1906).

Bibliography

Books

Aiken, George, ed. *The Great Locomotive Chase: As Told by Men Who Made It Happen*. Gatlinburg, TN: Historic Press South, 1994.

Armistead, Gene C. *Horses and Mules in the Civil War: A Complete History with a Roster of Over Seven Hundred War Horses*. Jefferson, NC: McFarland Publishing Co., 2013.

Arp, Bill, So Called [Charles Henry Smith]. *A Side Show of the Southern Side of the War*. New York: Metropolitan Record Office, 1866.

Aycock, Roger. *All Roads to Rome*. Rome, AL: Roger Aycock, 1981.

Basler, Roy P., ed. *The Collected Works of Abraham Lincoln*. Vol. 6. Brunswick, NJ: Rutgers University Press, 1953.

Battey, George M., Jr. *A History of Rome and Floyd County*. Atlanta: Webb and Vary, 1922.

Black, Robert C., III. *The Railroads of the Confederacy*. Chapel Hill: University of North Carolina Press, 1952.

Blount County Historical Society. *The Forrest-Streight Raid: A Blount County Viewpoint*. N.p., 1963.

Bonds, Russell S. *Stealing the General: The Great Locomotive Chase and the First Medal of Honor*. Yardley, PA: Westholme Publishers, 2007.

Botkin, B.A. *A Civil War Treasury of Tales, Legends, and Folklore*. New York: Random House, 1960.

Bradley, Michael P. *Nathan Bedford Forrest's Escort and Staff*. Gretna, LA: Pelican Publishing Company, Inc., 2008.

Brown, Barry L., and Gordon R. Elwell. *Crossroads of Conflict: A Guide to Civil War Sites in Georgia*. Athens: Georgia Civil War Commission, the University of Georgia Press, 2010.

Brown, Campbell H., ed. *Reminiscences of Newton Cannon, First Sergeant, C.S.A.* Jackson, TN: McCowat-Mercer Press, Inc., 1963.

Brown, Joseph E. *The Confederate Records of the State of Georgia: Official Correspondence of Governor Joseph E. Brown*. Atlanta: Charles R. Byrd, State Publisher, 1910.

———. *Report of the Superintendent and Treasurer of the Western & Atlantic Railroad, 1862*. Atlanta: Woodruff Library, Emory University, n.d.

Bryan, Thomas Conn. *Confederate Georgia*. Athens: University of Georgia Press, 1953.

Clark, John E., Jr. *Railroads in the Confederacy: The Impact of Management on Victory and Defeat*. Baton Rouge: Louisiana State University Press, 2001.

Cleveland, Henry. *Alexander H. Stephens in Public and Private, with Letters and Speeches Before, During, and Since the War*. Atlanta: National Publishing Co., 1866.

Committee of the Seventy-Third Indiana Regimental Association. *History of the Seventy-Third Indiana Volunteers*. Washington, D.C.: Carnahan Press, 1909.

Cooper, William J., ed. *Jefferson Davis: The Essential Writings*. New York: Random House, 2003.

Cozzens, Peter. *The Darkest Days of the War: The Battles of Iuka and Corinth*. Chapel Hill: University of North Carolina Press, 1991.

Daniel, Larry J. *Days of Glory: The Army of the Cumberland, 1861–1865*. Baton Rouge: Louisiana State University Press, 2004.

———. *Soldiering in the Army of Tennessee: A Portrait of Life in a Confederate Army*. Chapel Hill: University of North Carolina Press, 1991.

Danielson, Joseph W. *War's Desolating Scourge: The Union's Occupation of North Alabama*. Lawrence: University Press of Kansas, 2012.

Davis, Stephen M. *What the Yankees Did to Us: Sherman's Bombardment and Wrecking of Atlanta*. Macon, GA: Mercer University Press, 2012.

Downing, David. *A South Divided*. Nashville, TN: Cumberland House, 2007.

Duncan, Thomas A. *Recollections of Thomas A. Duncan, Confederate Soldier*. Nashville, TN: McQuiddy Printing Co., 1922.

Fisher, John E. *They Rode with Forrest and Wheeler: A Chronicle of Five Tennessee Brothers' Service in the Confederate Western Cavalry*. Jefferson, NC: McFarland and Co., 1995.

Fulenwider, Dan, and Smokey. *Civil War: Stories of North Alabama and the South.* Cullman, AL: Blalock Publishing, 1998.

Garfield, James A. *The Wild Life of the Army: Civil War Letters of James A. Garfield.* Edited by Frederick W. Williams. Lansing: Michigan State University Press, 1961.

Garrison, Webb. *Atlanta and the War.* Nashville, TN: Rutledge Hill Press, 1995.

Glazner, John Frank. *Geography of the Great Appalachian Valley of Alabama.* Lancaster, PA: Science Press Printing Co., 1938.

Hartpence, William Ross. *History of the Fifty-First Indiana Veteran Volunteer Infantry: A Narrative of Its Organization, Marches, Battles and Other Experiences in Camp and Prison, from 1861–1866.* Indianapolis, IN: R. Clarke, 1894.

Henry, Robert Selph, ed. *As They Saw Forrest: Some Recollections and Comments of Contemporaries.* Jackson, TN: McCowat-Mercer Press, Inc., 1956.

———. *"First with the Most" Forrest.* New York: Bobbs-Merrill Co., 1944.

Hergesheimer, Joseph. *Swords and Roses.* New York: A.A. Knopf, 1929.

Hess, Earl J. *The Civil War in the West: Victory and Defeat from the Appalachians to the Mississippi.* Chapel Hill: University of North Carolina Press, 2012.

Hirshson, Stanley P. *Grenville M. Dodge.* Bloomington: Indiana University Press, 1967.

Jackson, Olin. *Tales of the Rails in Georgia.* Roswell, GA: Legacy Communications, Inc., 2004.

Johnston, James H. *Western and Atlantic Railroad of the State of Georgia.* Atlanta: Stine Printing Co., 1931.

Jones, Archer. *Confederate Strategy from Shiloh to Vicksburg.* Baton Rouge: Louisiana State University Press, 1991.

Jordan, Thomas, and J.P. Pryor. *The Campaigns of General Nathan Bedford Forrest and of Forrest's Cavalry.* New York: DaCapo Press, 1996.

Lamers, William M. *The Edge of Glory: A Biography of General William S. Rosecrans.* New York: Harcourt, Brace and World, 1961.

Marshall, Lamar, Larry Smith, and Michael Wren. *Alabama Collection Camps, Forts, Emigrating Depots and Travel Routes Used During the Cherokee Removal, 1838–1839.* Carol King, Project Director, National Park Service. Muscle Shoals, AL: Northwest Shoals Community College, Southeast Anthropological Institute, March 1909.

McMillan, Malcolm C. *The Alabama Confederate Reader.* Tuscaloosa: University of Alabama Press, 1963.

McMurry, Richard M. *Two Great Rebel Armies: An Essay in Confederate Military History.* Chapel Hill: University of North Carolina Press, 1989.

McWhiney, Grady. *Braxton Bragg and Confederate Defeat*. Vol. 1. Tuscaloosa: University of Alabama Press, 1964.

Minor, Craig. *A Most Magnificent Machine: America Adopts the Railroad, 1825–1862*. Lawrence: University Press of Kansas, 2010.

Morton, John Watson. *The Artillery of Nathan Bedford Forrest's Cavalry: "The Wizard of the Saddle."* Kennesaw, GA: Continental Book Co., 1962 (previously published Nashville and Dallas: Publishing House of the M.E. Church, South, 1909).

Nowland, John H.B. *Sketches of Prominent Citizens of 1876: With a Few of the Pioneers of the City and County Who Have Passed Away*. Indianapolis, IN: Tilford and Cadon, 1877.

Prince, Richard E. *Nashville, Chattanooga & St. Louis Railway History and Steam Locomotives*. Bloomington: Indiana University Press, 2001.

Reynolds, Hughes. *The Coosa River Valley*. Cynthiana, KY: Hobson Print Press, 1991.

Roach, Alva C. *The Prisoner of War, and How Treated*. Indianapolis, IN: Railroad City Publishing House, A.D. Streight, Proprietor, 1865.

Roland, Charles P. *An American Iliad: The Story of the Civil War*. New York: McGraw Hill, 1991.

Russell, James M. *Atlanta 1847–1890: City Building in the Old South and New*. Baton Rouge: Louisiana State University Press, 1988.

Starnes, H. Gerald. *Forrest's Forgotten Horse Brigadier*. Bowie, MD: Heritage Press, 1995.

Storey, Margaret M. *Loyalty and Loss: Alabama Unionists in the Civil War and Reconstruction*. Baton Rouge: Louisiana State University Press, 2004.

Streight, Abel D. *The Crisis of Eighteen Hundred and Sixty-One in the Government of the United States: Its Cause, and How It Should Be Met*. Indianapolis, IN: A.D. Streight, 1861. Gutenberg e-book, http://www.gutenberg.org/files/38454.

Taliaferro, Tevi. *Historic Oakland Cemetery*. Charleston, SC: Arcadia Publishing, 2001.

Todd, Glenda McWhirter. *First Alabama Cavalry, U.S.A.: Homage to Patriotism*. Bowie, MD: Heritage Books, 1999.

Turner, George Edgar. *Victory Rode the Rails: The Strategic Place of the Railroads in the Civil War*. Lincoln: University of Nebraska Press, 1992.

U.S. War Department. *The War of the Rebellion: A Compilation of the Official Records of the Union and Confederate Armies*. 128 vols. Washington, D.C.: Government Printing Office, 1880–1901.

Walsh, George. *Those Damn Horse Soldiers: True Tales of the Civil War Cavalry.* New York: Tom Doherty Associates, 2006.

Willett, Robert L., Jr. *The Lightning Mule Brigade: Abel Streight's 1863 Raid into Alabama.* Carmel, IN: Gould Press, 1999.

Wills, Brian Steel. *A Battle from the Start: The Life of Nathan Bedford Forrest.* New York: Harper and Collins, 1997.

W.K. Dickson & Co., Inc. *The Georgia Civil War Heritage Trail System.* Atlanta: W.K. Dickson & Co., Inc., 2001.

Wyeth, John Allan, MD, LLD. *Life of Lieutenant-General Nathan Bedford Forrest.* New York and London: Harper & Brothers, 1908. (The book was previously published in 1899 by Harper & Brothers, and it was subsequently published in 1975 by Press of Morningside Bookshop with a slight variation in the title. The book was published as *That Devil Forrest: Life of General Nathan Bedford Forrest* by Louisiana State University Press in 1989. There have been several editions since with various co-authors and variations in the title.)

———. *That Devil Forrest: Life of General Nathan Bedford Forrest.* Baton Rouge: Louisiana State University Press, 1989. (The book was originally published as *Life of Lieutenant-General Nathan Bedford Forrest*, New York: Harper & Brothers, 1899. Subsequent editions include one in 1908 by Harper & Brothers and one in 1975 by Press of Morningside Bookshop, with slight variations in the title. There have been several editions since with various co-authors and variations in the title.)

Articles

Agee, Rucker. "Forrest-Streight Campaign of 1863." Preliminary report prepared for the 100th meeting of the Civil War Round Table of Milwaukee, Wisconsin, June 26, 1958.

Aycock, Roger. "John Wisdom's Ride Made Him Georgia's Paul Revere." *Rome (GA) News-Tribune*, June 24, 1973.

———. "Two Famous Rides Compared." *Rome News-Tribune*, October 19, 1996.

Bearss, Edwin. "Colonel Streight Drives for the Western and Atlantic Railroad." *Alabama Historical Quarterly* 26 (1961): 133–86.

Black, Robert C., III. "The Railroads of Georgia in the Confederate War Effort." *Journal of Southern History* 13, no. 4 (November 1947): 511–34.

Bogle, James G. "Civil War Railroads—Georgia and Tennessee." *The Atlanta Historical Bulletin* 12, no. 3 (Fall 1967): 23–37.

Cofield, John, "William Faulkner and the Mule Picture." http://hottytoddy.com/2013/02/01/william-faulkner-and-the-mule-picture. February 1, 2013.

"A Company Made Favor with Gen. Forrest." *Confederate Veteran* 22 (March 1914): 130–31.

Cook, James E. "The 1863 Raid of Abel Streight: Why It Failed." *Alabama Review* 20 (October 1961): 254–69.

Crawford, Charles W. "A Note on Forrest's Race for Rome." *Georgia Historical Quarterly* 50 (1966): 288–90.

Crownover, Danny. "Exploit of the Murphree Sisters." *The Vagabond*, http://www.GadsdenMessenger.com, December 5, 2014/6B.

Dinkins, James. "Forrest's Pursuit and Capture of Colonel Streight." *Confederate Veteran* (December 1925): 452–54, and (January 1926): 15–18.

"51st Indiana Infantry in the American Civil War." http://www.civilwarindex.com/armyin/51st_in_infantry.html.

Gadsden Times. "R.C. Garrett Witnessed Emma Sansom's Deed." August 17, 1958.

———. "William Alfred Williams and Emma Sansom." July 18, 1951.

Gates, Frederick B. "Notes and Documents: The Impact of the Western & Atlantic Railroad on the Development of the Georgia Upcountry, 1840–1860." *Georgia Historical Quarterly* 91, no. 2 (Summer 2007): 169–84.

Grabau, Warren Edward. "'It Will Be a Terrible Blow': Streight's Raid Across North Alabama, 8 April–4 May, 1863." Jackson: Mississippi Department of Archives and History, 2003, n.p.

Hebert, Keith S. "Streight's Raid." www.encyclopediaofalabama.org/article/h-1380.

Hoggman, Brett. "Hunting Yankees—Brigadier General Nathan Bedford Forrest and the Streight Raid in Northern Alabama 1863." Scandinavian Center for Research on Confederate Guerrilla and Partisan Raiding 1861–1865 (February 1993): Paper no. 11, 2–5.

Jacksonville (AL) Republican. "Gen. Forrest in Rome." Vol. 27, no. 17, May 9, 1863.

Leigh, Phil. "The Great Locomotive Chase." http://www.opinionator.blogs.nytimes.com/?s=great+locomotive+chase), April 13, 2012.

McCash, William Barton. "Colonel Abel D. Streight's Raid, His Capture and Imprisonment." Master's thesis, University of Georgia, 1956.

Monroe, H.G. "Chattanooga Choo-Choo and Diesels." *Railroad Magazine* 27, no. 2 (November 1948): 12–39.

Owen, Thomas McAdory. "Emma Sansom: An Alabama Heroine." Address delivered to the Sixth Annual Convention of the Alabama Division of the United Daughters of the Confederacy, in Demopolis,

Alabama, May 14, 1902. *Gulf States Historical Magazine* 2 (Birmingham, March–May 1904): 3–10.

Passenger timetable. March 1861. http://www.csa-railroads.com/index.htm.

Phillips, Ulrich B. "An American State-Owned Railroad: The Western and Atlantic." *Yale Review* 15, no. 3 (November 1906): 259–70.

Polites, Taylor M. "The Bloody Occupation of Northern Alabama." http://www.opinionator.blogs.nytimes.com/?s=bloody+occupation, February 28, 2013.

Reynolds, Clark G. "Confederate Romans and Bedford Forrest." *Georgia Historical Quarterly*, no. 1 (Spring 1993): 20–40.

Ricci, Joseph A. "Captain Dinkins in War and Peace." *Memorial Hall Foundation Newsletter* (Summer 2016): 1–7.

Stokes, David M. "Railroads Blue and Gray: Rail Transport in the War 1861–1865: A Bibliography." *National Railway Bulletin* 65, no. 5 (2000): 4–11, 32–37.

"The Story of Roderick." http://www.roderickplace.com/history.html, n.d.

Taylor, R.N. *Gadsden Times*, August 17, 1958.

"W&A Railroad Tunnel." http://www.tunnelhillheritagecenter.com/#!tunnel, n.d.

"Western and Atlantic Railroad." http://www.aboutnorthgeorgia.com/ang/Western_and_Atlantic_Railroad, n.d.

"Western & Atlantic Railroad." http://www.ourgeorgiahistory.com/ogh/Western_and_Atlantic_Railroad, n.d.

"Western and Atlantic Railroad in the Civil War." http://www.aboutnorthgeorgia.com/ang/Western_and_Atlantic_Railroad_in_the_Civil_War, n.d.

"Western & Atlantic Railroad Zero Milepost." http://www.nps.gov/nr/travel/atlanta/wes.htm, n.d.

Whitsitt, W.H. "A Year with Forrest." *Confederate Veteran* 25, no. 10 (August 1917): 357–62.

Wilson, John. "Chattanooga Railroad Series: The Old Line of the Western and Atlantic Railroad." http://www.chattanoogan.com/2013/12/26/266104/Chattanooga-Railroad-Series-The-Old.aspx, December 26, 2013.

Wilson, R.D. "The Mule Brigade and 'That Devil Forrest.'" http://www.home.comcast.net/~edwilson10/STREIGHT.doc.pdf.

Witherspoon, J.G. "Confederate Cavalry Leaders." *Confederate Veteran* 27, no. 11 (November 1919): 414–17.

Encyclopedias and Anthologies

Bryan, Charles F. "Chattanooga." In *Encyclopedia of the Confederacy*. Vol. 1. New York: Simon and Schuster, 1993.

Buell, Don Carlos. "Operations in North Alabama." In *Battles and Leaders of the Civil War*. Vol. 2. Robert Underwood Johnson and Clarence Clough Buel, eds. New York: Thomas Yoseloff, Inc., 1956.

Degler, Carl. "Unionism." In *Encyclopedia of the Confederacy*. Vol. 4. New York: Simon and Schuster, 1993.

Pittenger, William. "The Locomotive Chase in Georgia." In *Battles and Leaders of the Civil War*. Vol. 2. Robert Underwood Johnson and Clarence Clough Buel, eds. New York: Thomas Yoseloff, Inc., 1956.

Roach, Alva C. "Notes from the Other Side." In *As They Saw Forrest: Some Recollections and Comments of Contemporaries*, Robert Selph Henry. Jackson, TN: McCowat-Mercer Press, Inc., 1956.

Speed, Thomas. "Cavalry Operations in the West under Rosecrans and Sherman." In *Battles and Leaders of the Civil War*. Vol. 4. New York: Thomas Yoseloff, 1956.

Stover, John. "Railroads." In *Encyclopedia of the Confederacy*. Vol. 3. New York: Simon and Schuster, 1993.

Special Collections and Contributions

Rucker Agee, letter. N.d. Courtesy of Norwood Kerr. Mississippi Department of Archives and History. Montgomery, AL.

Bragg to Shorter. May 6, 1863. Southern Telegraph Co. Mississippi Department of Archives and History. Montgomery, AL.

Stanton J. Brumfield letter to wife, Mary Jane. April 20, 1863. Indianapolis: Indiana Historical Society.

Norman Dasinger Jr. Streight's Raid–Forrest's Pursuit timeline.

Thomas Hoffman diary. State Historical Society of Iowa. Cited in Joseph W. Danielson's *War's Desolating Scourge*, 120.

Larry Johnson, Emma Sansom's great-grandson. Personal collection.

Mary Harrison Lister collection. Typescript copy of article in the *Gadsden Times*, November 26, 1939, by Mary Harrison Lister about Emma Sansom. Also letter to Mary Harrison Lister from Mrs. J.B. McKinnon, formerly Mary Blair, Emma's friend, December 1, 1939, describing the events of May 2, 1863. Also civic publication, "The Home of Emma Sansom, Heroine of the Southern Confederacy, Invites the

WAC (Womens' Army Corps) to Gadsden, Alabama" (Gadsden, 1954). Gadsden Public Library, Gadsden, AL.

Will Martin collection. February 21, 1947. Gadsden Public Library. Gadsden, AL.

John McKee diary. 2nd Iowa Infantry, 1863–1864. United States Army Heritage and Education Center. Carlisle, PA.

William Spencer collection (SC1387). Memoir. "My Capture: Seven Months in Libby Prison." Indianapolis: Indiana Historical Society.

About the Author

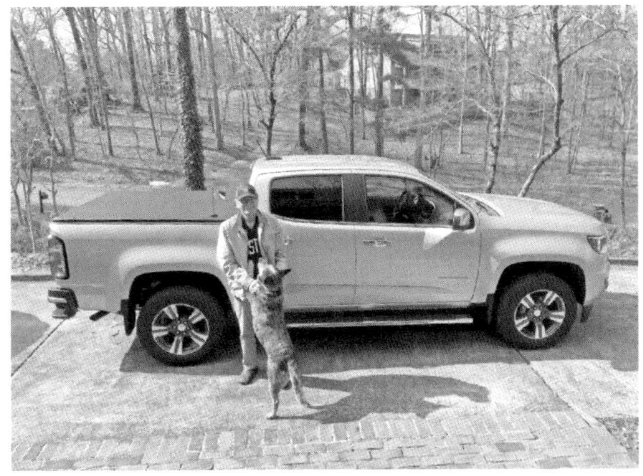

Dr. Brandon H. Beck is Director Emeritus of the McCormick Civil War Institute at Shenandoah University in Winchester, Virginia, which established Civil War scholarship in the Shenandoah Valley. He is the author of ten books, including histories and guide books of the three battles of Winchester. He edited the memoir of General Cullen Andrews Battle, *Third Alabama!*, for the University of Alabama Press. Since retiring and moving to Columbus, Mississippi, he has written two books for The History Press: *The Battle of Okolona: Defending the Mississippi Prairie* and *Holly Springs: Earl Van Dorn, the CSS* Arkansas, *and the Raid That Saved Vicksburg*. This is his third book for The History Press. He currently teaches courses on the history of Western Civilization at East Mississippi Community College. He is shown here with his Mississippi blue heeler, Champ.